W9-BZG-943

Reflective Practice for Educators

Improving Schooling Through Professional Development

Reflective Practice for Educators

Improving Schooling Through Professional Development

Karen F. Osterman
Robert B. Kottkamp

CORWIN PRESS, INC.
A Sage Publications Company
Newbury Park, California

For information address:

Corwin Press, Inc.
SAGE Publications, Inc.
2455 Teller Road
Thousand Oaks, California 91320
E-mail: order@sagepub.com

SAGE Publications Ltd.
6 Bonhill Street
London EC2A 4PU
United Kingdom

SAGE Publications India Pvt. Ltd.
M-32 Market
Greater Kailash I
New Delhi 110 048 India

Printed in the United States of America

Library of Congress Cataloging-in-Publication Data

Osterman, Karen F.
  Reflective practice for educators : improving schooling though professional development / Karen F. Osterman, Robert B. Kottkamp.
    p. cm.
  Includes bibliographical references (p.) and index.
  ISBN 0-8039-6046-8. —ISBN 0-8039-6047-6 (pbk.)
  1. Teachers—In-service training—United States. 2. School administartors—In-service training—United States. 3. School improvement programs—United States. 4. Learning. 5. Teaching. I. Kottkamp, Robert B. II. Title.
LB1731.O78 1993
371.1'46—dc20   92-37083

The paper in this book meets the specifications for permanence of the American National Standards Institute and the National Association of State Textbook Administrators.

    99 00 01 02 08 07 06 05 04

Corwin Press Production Editor: Tara S. Mead

Contents

Preface

We have written this book out of our deep concern for improving education. To improve education, we must change schools. To improve schools, we must change individuals. To improve individuals, we must change the ways we attempt to create change.

For more than a decade, this nation has been awash in demands that schools improve and in proposals and mandates to bring about desired changes. Governors, legislatures, policy experts, and blue ribbon commissions have proposed and executed reforms. Yet, too little has changed with our schools and their outcomes. What most of these reform attempts have shared is external origin and design and top-down, uniform, by-the-numbers application. Further, most reform attempts have provided no voice or creative role for the professional individuals who must carry them out if any change is to occur. We believe that reflective practice, an approach to educational improvement that is both situation specific and places the professional in the very center of the attempt to create improvement, not only stands in contrast to most other current ideas but has the greatest potential of any approach for improving individuals and, through them, schools and education.

We have written this book not just because we share an intellectual interest in reflection but because we share a passionate commitment to the process we believe has the best hope of bringing about significant and needed change. As university professors in a professional preparation program, reflective practice has been our own way of finding a deeply personal link between theory and our professional practice, between professing and taking personal action to improve the quality of U.S. public education. We are true believers in this process, not in the sense that we have found "the answer," but in the sense that here is an approach to personal and organizational change and improvement that is open ended, that encourages us to continue learning and growing ourselves at the same time that it enhances the professional development of our students and colleagues, and that holds tremendous potential for working out specific improvements in very different educational organizations and contexts. We have written with the sense that what we have set down is not an end but both a beginning to our own continued development in working with and through reflective practice and the beginning of personal journeys of experimentation and development that our work may spawn among our readers.

We also have written this book because while (unfortunately, in our view) *reflection* and *reflective practice* have become buzzwords, there is a dearth of resources to make this process readily available for use by individuals who are not already experts in the method. There is a widespread need for more information on the concept and its application, particularly because the reflective practice model of professional education stands in sharp contrast to many of the assumptions shaping the traditional models currently in use. And, while there are numerous articles and a few books on reflective practice, there is a need for a single source that, while focusing on the doing and facilitating of reflective practice, also grounds the "how to" in a solid conceptual base. Because the vast majority of what has been written also focuses on preservice teacher education, there is also a need for a source describing specific application of the process to educational administration and to improving the work of practicing educators.

This book is intended as a conceptually based practical guide to reflective practice for educators at any level who are committed to improving the quality of education and want to improve their own professional development abilities as a means toward that end: for university faculty members who wish to incorporate reflective practice methods into formal academic programs, for teachers who wish to engage in reflective practice with their students or colleagues, and for administrators who wish to develop more effective supervisory skills. Echoing Griffiths's (1979) position that education must be grounded in the ordinary experiences of individual people and expressed in ordinary language, we have attempted to explain conceptual terms in simple language and to illustrate these concepts using examples drawn from everyday experience.

Writing this book has been a growth-producing and reflective venture for us. For periods of 5 and a dozen years, respectively, each of us had developed a particular and different approach to teaching and facilitating reflection before beginning formal collaboration in writing. Writing has made us clarify conceptual issues and confront and define problems that were only vague awarenesses before we began. We have learned a great deal from each other as we personally went through reflective processes in the work of writing. We hope to save our readers some time and frustration by passing along what we have learned in the process of writing as well as in the process of facilitating reflective practice.

OVERVIEW

In Chapter 1, we explore the rationale for reflective practice, a professional development strategy whose objective is behavioral change. Professionals engage in reflective practice to develop a new awareness of their own performance and to improve the quality of their practice. This first chapter discusses the importance of personal change as a means to organizational change. *Improving Schools from Within* reflects Barth's (1990) belief that principals and teachers can learn new ways of working together and create schools that work for people. This chapter takes the same perspective that educators have the power to transform schools, and it explains how reflective practice facilitates individual and organizational change.

While Chapter 1 explores reflective practice within a social and organizational context, Chapter 2 focuses directly on reflective practice as a professional development process. Presenting the argument that reflective practice is a nontraditional approach to professional development that requires new conceptual and technical approaches to learning and instruction, we begin the chapter by contrasting the beliefs, assumptions, and strategies of reflective practice with traditional approaches to professional development. The second section of this chapter provides a conceptual answer to the question: What do we mean by reflective practice and how does it work? The process is described within the tradition of experiential learning.

With the conceptual framework established, Chapters 3 and 4 offer general guidelines for engaging in reflective practice. Beginning with the assumption that trust is a basic and critical element, Chapter 3 focuses on the role of the facilitator in establishing a supportive environment conducive to reflection and growth. Chapter 4 outlines various methods of creating or re-creating important aspects of professional practice as a means to identify the personal action theories that shape behavior.

The next three chapters describe reflective practice in action. By describing our personal experiences with reflective practice in different situations and settings, we hope to explore and illustrate reflective practice in meaningful ways: What is it like from the perspective of the facilitator and the participants? How does it unfold in varying and often unpredictable ways? What is the impact it has on the participants? In Chapter 5, Kottkamp reviews his work over a 12-year period introducing administrators and prospective administrators to reflective practice through a graduate course: "The Reflective Administrator." In Chapter 6, Osterman describes her work with a small group of experienced New York City public school principals as part of a semester-long professional development program designed to improve school leadership. In Chapter 7, Kottkamp depicts a Long Island school district's experiment in reflective practice, an ongoing and evolving reflective conversation among superintendent, central office administrators, school principals, and university researchers.

The final chapter examines impact: Does reflective practice work, and, if so, why? What accounts for the apparently significant and long-lasting effects? In addressing these questions, we identify key aspects of the process and discuss reflective practice as an empowering and motivational process that enhances individual and organizational performance.

ACKNOWLEDGMENTS

Perhaps more than most, this book could not have been written without the support of many people. It is customary for professors to acknowledge the contribution of their students. In our case, our students were the very medium in which the ideas and practices were learned and developed. This is not a book we wrote or could have written in a library. It required years of rolled-up-sleeves interaction with learners in a mutual pursuit of understanding. To all our students and colleagues at Hofstra and Rutgers Universities, the Professional Development Center, and the Administrative Reflection Group who taught us in ways some know and others will never know, we say many thanks.

For many years, our work has been supported by the happy accident of our membership in the Department of Administration and Policy Studies of the School of Education, Hofstra University. Support here has come less from specific discussion of the ideas we were working on than from the environment it provided us. This special group of people has created the best workplace example of Model II assumptions and behaviors that we have experienced. It is a group in which our assumptions, values, and the ideas of reflective practice have been nurtured and probed. It is a group that has enabled us to be more reflective practitioners through our everyday collaborations with them. We are fortunate to have you as colleagues. Thank you Donna Barnes, Pat Brieschke, Ley Browder, Karen Michaelis, Mary Anne Raywid, Charol Shakeshaft, Leslie Siskin, and Tim Smith.

We received special personal support and intellectual stimulation from Hofstra colleagues Janet Miller and Michael O'Laughlin, both pioneers in reflective practice in their own right. Janet's special contributions to the existence and success of the Administrative Reflection Group and our learning from it are evident in the content of Chapter 7. We both benefited significantly from our work with Susan Sullivan of the Professional Development Center. With her support, we learned a great deal about reflection with involuntary participants.

Chuck Achilles and Bruce Barnett, who are both deeply committed to improving the quality of professional preparation of educational administrators through their own personal quests and who have an uncommon appreciation of what we are attempting to do in our work, provided us with rapid, insightful, useful, and critically reflective responses to our first draft. The result is better because they listened deeply and told us where we were asking our readers to do too much reading between the lines.

Gracia Alkema had faith in us from the beginning and kept it as we blew deadlines at the end and struggled to get the book "really right." We were blessed with an individual who, having edited some of Argyris and Schon's early work, appreciated the power and value of the ideas we were working with in a way that few authors experience from their editors.

Most important, we are grateful for our supportive families. Our spouses, David and Ginny, and our children, Sunshine, Heather, Charlie, and Sam, and Nathan and Jeremy, helped us to carve out the space and the time to engage in writing, always a very selfish act in terms of family. We appreciate your forbearance, your faith in us, and your numerous implicit and explicit displays of support, especially Heather's valuable editing and Sam's astute observations on the nature of schooling. Thank you!

Karen F. Osterman
Robert B. Kottkamp

About the Authors

Karen F. Osterman is Assistant Professor of Administration and Policy Studies at Hofstra University. Her teaching, research, consulting, and publications reflect dual interests in reflective practice as a means of professional development and organizational change and problems of practice within the principalship. After receiving her Ph.D. in Educational Policy Planning and Administration from Washington University in 1984, she was Assistant Director of a regional principal center until assuming her position at Hofstra in 1987. As Director of the Silver Center for Reflective Principals from 1989 to 1991, she worked closely with principals, school districts, and university faculty on a national and international basis to support the use of reflective practice as a means of improving practice in the principalship. Related articles have appeared in *Education and Urban Society, Planning and Changing,* and the *Journal of School Leadership.* She is currently engaged in curricular reform efforts within the administrative preparation program at Hofstra and continues her professional development work with experienced principals. Ongoing research efforts address the problems and perspectives of new principals in New York City and supervisory communication within the school context.

Robert B. Kottkamp taught in a Missouri high school for 9 years. On completion of his Ph.D. at Washington University in St. Louis, he began his academic career at Rutgers University. He is currently Associate Professor and directs the doctoral program in the Department of Administration and Policy Studies at Hofstra University. He has written *To Be a Teacher* (1986) with Marilyn M. Cohn and Eugene F. Provenzo, Jr.; *Open Schools/Healthy Schools: Measuring Organizational Climate* (1990) with Wayne K. Hoy and C. J. Tartar; and *Teachers: The Missing Voice in Education* (1992) with Marilyn M. Cohn. He has published articles in *Phi Delta Kappan, Educational Administration Quarterly, The Journal of Research and Development in Education, The Alberta Journal of Educational Research, Education and Urban Society, The Journal of Educational Measurement,* and other journals. He has been active in the American Educational Research Association and has represented two universities at the University Council for Educational Administration. He recently received the Robert S. Guttchen Memorial Distinguished Faculty Service Award from his School of Education colleagues. One current activity (with department colleagues) is revising the doctoral program with the assistance of a Danforth Foundation grant to support reform of administrative preparation. Reflection is a key component in this work.

1

Reflective Practice: A Powerful Force for Educational Change

Reflective practice is a powerful approach to professional development. But it is much more. It is an integrated way of thinking and acting focused on learning and behavioral change; it is individuals working to improve organizations through improving themselves.

In this chapter, we explore the relationship between reflective practice and educational change. Reflective practice is based on the beliefs that organizational change begins with us, that unless we change behaviors organizations will not change, and that many blocks to change are rooted in unexamined assumptions guiding our stable behavioral patterns. To create change, then, we must examine our own behaviors carefully, bring unexamined assumptions to awareness, and consciously self-monitor both our behaviors and our assumptions.

We begin by examining the failure of most educational change and reform efforts. Within this context, the balance of the chapter explores the reflective practice view of why change is difficult and how it may be brought about.

1

THE FAILURE OF EDUCATIONAL
CHANGE AND REFORM EFFORTS

Tenacious and Ubiquitous Problems

In this nation, we have one solid consensus: The educational system is not meeting our expectations. Many individuals and groups have, with goodwill, developed and prescribed seemingly sensible ideas for improving and reforming schools. But, with all this concern and suggestion, the educational enterprise remains very stable in structure and operation. Much that characterized schools and teaching decades, or even a century, ago still characterizes education today. It's not that we haven't tried very hard to change things, but we just don't seem to succeed.

In 1990, the National Assessment of Educational Progress, for example, released a 20-year study of education ("Past and Future," 1991). It reported that, while there were gains in basic skills test scores, fewer students demonstrated a grasp of the higher-level thinking skills and fewer were enrolled in advanced-level courses.

Perhaps more distressing is the finding that how teachers teach students has not changed in important ways. Despite much research suggesting better alternatives, classrooms are still textbook and teacher lecture centered, and students spend much time completing short-answer activity sheets. They spend little school time actually reading, writing about and discussing what they read, thinking about issues with elusive answers, or working in independent activities or group projects (Cuban, 1984; Goodlad, 1984).

If little has changed in the classroom, the same can be said about administration. Despite a decade of intense dialogue about school restructuring, little has changed in the way schools are organized and operated. School administrators still tend to use the same hierarchical approaches found decades ago before there was so much attention, discussion, and legislation aimed at introducing collaborative approaches to management (Malen, Ogawa, & Kranz, 1990; Schmuck & Schmuck, 1990).

The French have a saying: "The more things change, the more they stay the same." Sarason (1971, 1990) has been arguing for 20 years that this is an apt summary of attempts to change education. But he has also spent a distinguished career trying to understand why this is so and to do something about it. He concludes that our mode of attempting educational change is flawed.

The "Fix-It" Model

What is that mode? In examining educational reform, a clear pattern emerges. In our homes or workplaces, when something goes wrong with the pipes or the fixtures, we call in the plumber, the outside expert. The plumber comes to fix the problem by replacing the worn-out parts or bringing in a whole new set of fixtures to replace the old. In schools, the reform process looks very much like this "fix-it" model. Our actions assume that, with new parts—more money, more time, better curriculum, higher standards, new tests—which are all things that can be changed by someone else—curriculum experts, the legislature, the taxpayer, the state education department, the school board, a specialist of some kind—things will work better. But they haven't.

The introduction of new math was typical of the way many attempts to improve curriculum—a part replacement—have fared. With the rise of national concern, university experts developed a structure-of-the-discipline approach to mathematics teaching (Bruner, 1963). To them, it was a sound, internally consistent, and effective instructional approach. Innovators introduced teachers to the method and materials through a process typical of most professional development and graduate education. Instructors provided teachers with information about the new curriculum much in the same way teachers taught their students. The result: New books were found in classrooms, but teachers continued to teach the old math (Sarason, 1971). This pattern typifies many curricular change attempts.

Recent legislated attempts at school reform share many similarities with older curricular change efforts. Legislators developed reform policies, mandates, and programs for schools. They distributed these to educators through memos, lengthy documents, and state department of education emissaries who conducted information sessions indistinguishable in process from those used in curricular change attempts. External experts defined and solved the problem; others then delivered the answer for implementation. Again, they emphasized information transfer: the intent of the reform and "how to do it"—the new part and how to install it. The result has been the same: It didn't work! The more things change, the more they stay the same —except, in these cases, more residual rules and accountability mechanisms were added to school organizations (Cohn & Kottkamp, 1992; Wise, 1979, 1988).

So, if the "fix-it" model doesn't work, why not? To begin with, the way we approach change is closely related to how we think about organizations. Experience with school reform to date suggests that our common conception of the school as an organization is consistent with Weber's (1947) ideas on bureaucracy. In this framework, organizations are viewed as highly rational, impersonal, and mechanistic systems operating according to clearly defined and relatively inflexible rules and regulations. We tend, perhaps unconsciously, to treat organizations the way deists thought of the universe—something set up by a larger power and left to run according to its own immutable laws.

No one would openly dispute that organizations consist of people —individuals who join together to pursue common purposes. Yet, within our customary bureaucratic orientation, individuals get lost in the shadow of "the system." In our unexamined thinking, the organization seems to assume a life of its own, separate and distinct from the life of its members, and it emerges as an anonymous, depersonalized, and all-powerful collective, accountable to none and subject to no one's authority. Within the system, individuals are submerged, invisible, and powerless, and the notion of change or reform usually consists of similarly mechanistic approaches—hiring outsiders to fix this and that, to add a bit of something here or there, or to inject a new idea or theory. We are told how to implement somebody else's solution to "our problem." But it isn't our problem. We didn't participate in finding it, and we aren't very committed to the imposed solution. We feel that what somebody is always deciding to "fix" is us. So, while the impersonal organizational machine rumbles on, we shrug it off and say things like: "You can't beat 'the system.' " "The more things change, the more they stay the same."

REFLECTIVE PRACTICE:
A DIFFERENT VIEW OF CHANGE AND REFORM

Individuals and Organizational Change

Reflective practice takes a more optimistic perspective toward change: Organizational change is possible and individuals have the power to create it. To accept this perspective, however, requires altering our customary thoughts and beliefs about organizations. Although bureaucratic organization and effectiveness are commonly assumed to go together, this is not necessarily the case. There are other highly effective forms of organization where hierarchy, depersonalization, and standardization play little part. Organic structure, for example, is the opposite of Weber's bureaucracy in almost every dimension, characterized instead by loose, informal working relationships among organizational members (Burns & Stalker, 1961). In organic organizations, rules are more flexible and are worked out to meet the needs of workers who all share responsibility for the quality of organizational functioning. In this alternative way of structuring work, responsibility and authority are widely shared. The membership no longer automatically assumes that the "top" knows better and has the right and responsibility to tell others how to do things.

This and other alternative ways of perceiving organizations place much greater than customary emphasis on the people who work within them. Although organizations certainly exert powerful influences on the people who inhabit them, in this way of thinking, organizations are human creations guided by human intentions and decisions (Greenfield, 1986, 1991). Thus, if organizations are human constructions, the people in them should be the ones to determine what is needed and how to bring about meeting those needs. Within this way of thinking, organizational change is a result of people changing themselves. If children are not learning, what is needed is not necessarily a standard "fix-it," such as a new set of materials, but perhaps a change in how we teach and how we manage.

This people-in-the-center concept of organizational change is grounded in another, not widely accepted, assumption: Many organizational problems are rooted in overlooked, traditionally accepted behavior patterns, or "behavioral regularities" (Sarason, 1971), that lie below the surface of our awareness. It is the aggregation of these individual behavioral patterns that constitutes the organizational status quo. Organizations won't change until we who populate them begin acting in other than our "regular" ways.

Yet, our behavioral regularities are tenacious. Even though our ideas—about teaching, about administration, about our relationships with parents and community—change, we continue to behave in the same old ways. Despite a stock of new knowledge and our best intentions and beliefs, we tend to resist change and to behave in very predictable ways. Despite the substantial body of research demonstrating the superiority of heterogeneous over homogeneous grouping, schools still track students among classes; and within classes many teachers still assign children to different ability groups for instruction. Despite a growing body of research demonstrating the effectiveness of collaborative decision making, many administrators resist involving staff in a meaningful way. Despite considerable evidence on the failure of "fix-it"-style change efforts, we continue to prescribe and attempt one "fix" after another. It seems very difficult to adopt new instructional, leadership, or change-facilitating behavior patterns even though we recognize the impotence of old approaches and accept the need for different ones. So, how do we understand this "we believe it but can't seem to do it" phenomenon?

The ideas undergirding reflective practice provide a relatively simple rationale for this resistance to change. Behavior is habitual. Further, unless we pay very close and direct attention to our behavior, it is unlikely we'll be able to change it.

Behavior becomes habitual through acculturation. As we grow from infants to adults, society shapes our understanding of how the world works. In the same way that traditional societies transmit certain assumptions and beliefs about childbirth, family, natural forces, and the relationship of human beings to the cosmos, so too does our culture transmit through the daily processes of living the assumptions, beliefs, and knowledge that shape our behavior. As adult members of that society, we no longer focus consciously on many of our behaviors or the assumptions that lie behind them.

A clear example of the force of cultural influence in creating habitual behavior is the schooling process itself. Educators are the most thoroughly socialized of all professional groups. Some begin their experience with school culture in infant day care. Others begin in kindergarten or nursery school and may continue until retirement and beyond. Through this lengthy and relatively consistent experience, complex sets of knowledge, assumptions, beliefs, and behaviors are ingrained in us so deeply that we are no longer aware of them, yet they guide even minute details of our daily work behaviors. Because of this deep acculturation, we act in very consistent and predictable ways. A careful observer can identify our behavioral regularities and the assumptions that lie beneath them.

We can see the power of acculturated school behaviors and assumptions quite early in child's play. Ask young children with school experience to play school. If we watch the youthful "teacher," we typically see a role portrayal—tone, words, and actions—that demonstrates a clear understanding of teachers' thought and action. If we analyze the child's behavior, we often find an amazing correspondence between the assumptions underlying it and Dewey's (1938a) description of schooling: The chief business of school is to transmit bodies of information and skills worked out in the past to the new generation. Accordingly, learning is largely the acquisition of what is already incorporated in books and in the heads of the elders. Toward this end, teachers are agents for communicating knowledge and skills, and "since the subject matter is handed down from the past, the attitude of 'pupils' must . . . be one of docility, receptivity, and obedience" (p. 18). The child exhibits the same teacher-centered approach to instruction now that predominated in 1890 (Cuban, 1984).

Through the process of imitation and acculturation, we also learn about administrative behavior. In role-play situations, teachers enrolled in administrative preparation programs readily adopt the hierarchical tone, attitude, and behavior they critique in practicing administrators. Quite clearly, we learn to do things the way they are usually done. But, unfortunately, the way they have always been done is not necessarily the best way or the way we might choose to do things if we really thought about it.

Other familiar examples come to mind. "Open House" is one. Teachers and administrators decry the lack of parent involvement, particularly that of parents of at-risk children. Yet, every year, schools repeat the same Open House strategy to attempt to get parents into the school. The date is set and notices are sent home. Even when Monday night football is avoided, only a few parents show up. Educators are dismayed again at the lack of parental concern. "The ones who come are the ones we don't need to see." The pattern seldom differs. Schools continue to schedule Open Houses and send notes home the same way—even though it is unsuccessful and even though there are more effective strategies for gaining parental involvement.

But, if our behavior is so predictable and so resistant to change, how can behavior change come about? Reflective practice, a professional development strategy for achieving behavioral change, is our answer. To understand how reflective practice facilitates behavioral change, however, we need to understand more of the conceptual framework and rationale behind it.

Understanding Action Theories

In the reflective practice concept, observable behavior—the decisions we make, the actions we take, the way we act—is governed by personal action theories. Typically, the word *theory* carries connotations of abstract ideas dealing with issues detached from the world of practice. In reflective practice, however, "theories" are linked closely with daily existence and experience. They are simply the ideas and assumptions we hold about how things should and do work. Everyone has action theories: Teachers have theories about discipline and instruction; administrators have theories about leadership and supervision; parents have theories about child raising and discipline;

change agents have theories about facilitating change. Some action theories are stated in formal language, others appear in aphorisms: "Spare the rod and spoil the child." "Learning should be fun."

In reflective practice, two distinct types of personal action theories are key to understanding behavioral stability and change: espoused theories and theories-in-use.

Espoused theories. Of the two kinds of personal theories, espoused theories are easier to understand. They are quite simply what we are able to say we think and believe. Espoused theories have two distinct characteristics: (a) They exist at a conscious level, and (b) they change with relative ease in response to new information or ideas. Individuals often emerge from professional development and graduate courses able to articulate new ideas and understandings. Their espoused theories change. And, because espoused theories reflect conscious ideas, intentions, and beliefs, if we want to know what they are, we simply ask. Responses to questions will likely indicate the individual's broad range of information and belief acquired through experience and formal education.

But, while we believe that our espoused theories guide our actions, this is often not the case. As the dotted line in Figure 1.1 shows, espoused theories do not directly influence behavior. Actions are often inconsistent with intentions, and new ideas do not always lead to new behaviors: We continue to track students while citing the research supporting heterogeneous grouping; we maintain hierarchical relationships and unilateral behavior while advocating collaboration.

Theories-in-use. These theories are a very different matter. They are elusive and difficult to identify yet far more powerful in influencing how we act. In much the same way that genetic structure influences our physiological development, these theories contain the assumptions and beliefs that actually guide our behavior. The solid line in Figure 1.1 illustrates the direct relationship between theories-in-use and behavior. In contrast to espoused theories, which exist at a conscious level and are easily changed, theories-in-use have distinctly opposite characteristics: (a) They are so deeply ingrained in our consciousness that we cannot easily articulate them, and (b)

Figure 1.1. A Conceptual Framework Underlying Reflective Practice

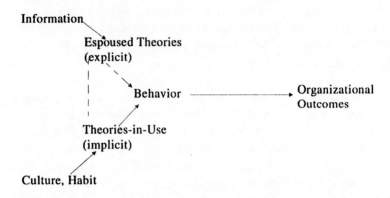

they are not easily changed (Argyris & Schon, 1974). But why are theories-in-use so difficult to know consciously, and what makes them difficult to alter? We have already seen the basic answer. Theories-in-use build up and solidify over a long period of time through acculturation and are reinforced by ongoing experience in the culture. They become such an integrated part of our beings that they are difficult to isolate. They disappear from our conscious "foreground" and become "background."

Language acquisition illustrates the nature of theories-in-use. We learn a native tongue through immersion, that is, acculturation. Through listening, imitating, practicing, and receiving feedback from others, we acquire a very complex set of assumptions, beliefs, and knowledge, or a theory-in-use for language. The knowledge component includes grammar, syntax, and vocabulary. We learn assumptions for interpreting meaning that come from the knowledge component as well as vocal and facial nuance, tone, volume, and other factors. By age 5 or so—no matter what our culture or language—we possess a very complex language theory-in-use that enables and governs verbal communication. But ask a 5-year-old to explain the grammar and syntax of something she just communicated and she is unable to do so. She has a theory-in-use for language, including its grammar, but no espoused theory that can be articulated. She knows a great deal but only in a way that is ineffable or that is "known-in-action," in the actual speaking and hearing of language (Schon, 1983). Much later in the schooling process, the contents of her theory-in-use for language will be made explicit through formal approaches to language such as learning grammar and perhaps diagraming sentences.

Another look at some prior illustrations also demonstrates theories-in-use. The child who can "play teacher" in a very convincing way or the teacher who can portray the administrator complete with body language and tone of voice are good examples. It is very unlikely that either the child or the teacher could explicitly describe all the details of their actions either before or after they complete them, yet they "know-in-action" in a very deep and complex way, a way that indicates the presence of a theory-in-use to regulate these particular aspects of life.

The recurrent behavior of teacher-centered instruction reflects certain teacher theory-in-use assumptions about the purpose of schooling and the nature of teaching and learning. We have theories-in-use for leadership; many of these contain assumptions about hierarchical position, being in charge, and being responsible for coming up with solutions to problems that we must define ourselves. We have theories-in-use for behavior in committee meetings, both as members and as the leader. As teachers, we have theories-in-use about classroom management and ways of dividing up students in groups for instruction. Our theories-in-use are functional in guiding the accomplishment of all these very complicated tasks and at the same time helping to conserve the conscious energy we are required to expend doing them. Our theories-in-use, however, also maintain behavioral regularities that are dysfunctional as well as those that are functional. Our theories-in-use keep us lecturing to students in groups, teaching math in the same way regardless of new methods and materials, and acting in noncollaborative ways as group leaders.

Many personal action theories, including theories-in-use, seem to be widely shared. Given that they develop from participation in a fairly stable and consistent culture, this makes sense. That theories-in-use are often shared also helps to explain why cultures remain stable. But the fact that individuals tend to share broad sets of assumptions and beliefs does not seem to make it any easier to describe our theories-in-use. Because they are so deeply ingrained and difficult to identify, they are particularly difficult to change.

Developing Awareness

Behavioral change comes about when new theories-in-use replace existing ones. Normally, we associate change with formal education. To foster change, we typically provide new information and new methods, and we assume that individuals will adopt new modes of behavior as a result. The reflective practice concept, however, challenges and modifies this assumption, maintaining that, while espoused theories readily incorporate new information, theories-in-use resist change. As we have seen, while we adopt new ideas, our behavior often continues unchanged.

One of the reasons that theories-in-use do not respond to new information is that in many cases we are simply unaware that a problem exists. We are unaware of discrepancies (a) between our beliefs (espoused theory) and actions (theory-in-use) or (b) between our actions and our intended outcomes. Without this awareness, the individual may not personalize the new information or ideas to make the connection between the criticism and his or her own behavior.

Discrepancies between espoused theories and theories-in-use. In the case of discrimination, for example, a person may denounce prejudicial behavior but fail to realize that he or she behaves in a discriminatory way. A school administrator may espouse the concept of collaborative management and not recognize autocratic aspects of his or her own behavior. A teacher may read the effective schools research and agree wholeheartedly on the importance of high expectations for all students and not see the inconsistency in having very high expectations for students perceived to be bright and having "adjusted" expectations for students with learning or behavioral problems. More troubling than these incongruities themselves is the fact that very often we are unaware of these intention-action incongruities. We simply do not see that our words and actions are not aligned —though it is easy for others to recognize this and think of us as inconsistent, hypocritical, or devious, which is not what we intend to be.

In these situations, a competing, deeply ingrained theory-in-use prevents the intention or new information (espoused theory) from holding sway. The administrator, for example, may find that his or her efforts to involve teachers in schoolwide decision making are in direct conflict with a theory-in-use containing the assumption that strong and effective leaders are responsible for making decisions and keeping things under control. Teachers who have different expectations for low- or underachieving students may have an embedded belief that maintaining high expectations for students who won't be able to perform at the same level as their more able counterparts will only create pressure and stress and further reduce their ability to learn.

Flawed theories and undesirable outcomes. Awareness of another type of discrepancy may be the stimulus for change. In some situations, observation may demonstrate a high level of consistency between espoused theories and theories-in-use: Assumptions and beliefs are synchronized with actions. The problem emerges when it becomes apparent that the theories are unsound; they simply don't yield the intended results. Just as professionals are often unaware of discrepancies between beliefs and actions, they are often blind to the impact of their actions. Take, for example, the principal who firmly believes that the only way to ensure quality is by regulating every aspect of teachers' performance. Consistent with this belief, and with the best interests of children in mind, the principal insists on a standardized format for instruction in the classroom and permits no divergence. While these actions may, in fact, lead to the desired standardization in curriculum and instruction, it is also likely that this strategy will deaden teachers' sense of professionalism, stifle creativity, and breed resentment and antagonism (Cohn & Kottkamp, 1992; Wise, 1988).

In the area of special education, we also see commonly accepted practice being challenged as new information and insight become available. Instructional techniques and materials have been developed ostensibly to meet the unique needs of children with learning difficulties. Because learning is such a difficult task for many of these children, educators have made an effort to simplify presentations, separating tasks into discrete elements. While these efforts were intended to facilitate learning by removing the complexity, they also may have created tasks that are so boring that they fail to engage the learners in any but a most superficial manner (Cummins, 1986).

In these examples, the beliefs and the actions corresponded. But, with a growing awareness of the full range of impact, the action theories proved to be ineffective. For change to take place, the individual must develop an understanding of his or her theories-in-use and at the same time become dissatisfied with the resulting performance. When the individual develops this conscious awareness of the relationship between a predominant theory-in-use and an unacceptable outcome, motivation to change is the usual result. Then, and only then, will possession of new information be useful in creating behavioral change. Without awareness, there will be no change.

But, if theories-in-use are so difficult to describe, how do we come to understand them at a conscious level? Although the assumptions and beliefs shaping our actions are deeply ingrained below the level of consciousness, they are implicit in our actions and can be made explicit through careful observation and analysis. Sarason (1971) illustrated the process of observation and analysis using the metaphor of a man from outer space who sat on a platform suspended above a school. Unable to understand the language, he could determine what was happening only by observing actions and events. Through observation, the space visitor identified certain behavioral regularities. He noted that some children leave one classroom and go to another for certain periods of time. The visitor also noted that, in many instances, these students were not present in their original classroom when new information was being presented there. By identifying these behavioral regularities, it becomes possible to explore the underlying assumptions, or theories-in-use, that guide teachers' actions by asking two basic questions: Were actions consistent with intentions? Were actions effective in achieving stated goals?

If the space visitor could communicate with the school personnel, he would likely discover major discrepancies between what they intended to accomplish and the impact of their actions. The children left the classroom to receive remedial instruction, ostensibly to bring them to the same level as the other students. Yet, this pull-out approach actually further increased the gap between the two groups of students because those in need of remediation regularly missed new information received by those remaining in the class and so continued to fall further behind them. These observable regularities in behavior, according to Sarason (1971), were so deeply ingrained in the culture of the school (and in the educators' theories-in-use) that few were actually aware of these patterns. Bringing the patterns of behavior to awareness, unearthing discrepancies between intentions and actions, illuminating the gap between vision and reality, and finding the problem set the stage for change and growth.

Recognizing the discrepancy between espoused beliefs and actions or between actions and outcomes often leads to a reexamination of the situation and the development of alternative approaches. In the last decade, for example, observations such as these have led to more conscious efforts to minimize disruption of instruction, to modify pull-out programs, and to increase time on task. In these cases, change resulted from a growing awareness of a discrepancy between intended outcomes and actual outcomes. The vision was finally seen as different than the reality, and this became a motivation to develop new action.

The following example also demonstrates how new information or a shift in perspective can lead to changes in beliefs about the best way to do things and also lead to behavioral change. Geriatric specialists found widespread use of tranquilizers and physical restraint among nursing home patients who had no physical or psychological problems to warrant their use. One such home is now drug and restraint free because of the director's insight. A geriatric specialist visited the residence and made a statement that nursing homes are like prisons for the residents because they are kept tied up and drugged up for the staff members' own convenience. The director, a nurse who had worked in the home for 11 years, reported getting angry and upset at the statement until she realized a few days later that the comment was valid. "I've been working here for all those years, and I've been tying people up and drugging them up and not even thinking about it." When she thought about it, she made the decision to change. She and the staff came up with creative solutions for residents' safety. Some patients now sleep in beanbag chairs or in beds only a few inches off the floor. Some patients stay up all night and sleep all day. Now, the director reports, care is designed with the patient—not the institution—in mind. The transformation was not expensive, but the savings were substantial. Savings on diapers alone amounted to $4,000 a year. Because staff were more involved with patients, absenteeism and turnover were down; residents were less depressed, more alert, and physically strong. People came in being unable to walk and, 3 months later, could walk several hundred feet by themselves. Following these changes, the director reported that people even left the nursing home to return to their own homes—something that seldom happened before (National Public Radio, 1991).

These examples illustrate the principle of change underlying reflective practice: Behavioral change occurs only when individuals discover a problem they accept as theirs. Through the process of observation and reflection, individuals become more sensitive to and more aware of their habitual patterns of behavior, the assumptions that shape their behavior, and the impact of their actions. In those cases where awareness highlights a problem—either a discrepancy between espoused theory and theory-in-use or a faulty theory—that awareness becomes the stimulus for change. A clearly defined problem, an apparent gap between the reality and the ideal, becomes an incentive for personal learning—an incentive to examine and modify one's own conscious and unconscious beliefs and assumptions about the nature of professional practice and an incentive to try new ways of doing things (Dewey, 1938b; Getzels, 1979; Senge, 1990). In the example above, the nursing director began to interpret the same situation in a different way. She developed a new perspective that gave her the courage and the incentive to try something different. Awareness is the basis for change.

SUMMARY

In this chapter, we set the context for describing reflective practice by presenting a conceptual framework for understanding behavioral stability and change. This framework differs considerably from the "fix-it" notion behind most attempts to create educational change and reform. It focuses attention on theories-in-use—action theories resulting from deep acculturation—as the basis for behavior and its stability. Behavioral change requires bringing the assumptions in these personal theories to consciousness so that new assumptions may be substituted and attempts at new behavior may be carefully monitored.

In Chapter 2, we provide definition and direct description of reflective practice, its concepts, assumptions, and practices. The focus is on the interrelationships of espoused theory, theory-in-use, behavior, and its results. For clarity, we also contrast the assumptions and practices of traditional staff development with those of reflective practice.

2 Rethinking Professional Development

In Chapter 1, we examined reflective practice through a wide-angle lens. The subject was a conceptual framework for understanding individual and organizational stability and change and the promise of reflective practice as a means of facilitating significant change.

In this chapter, we narrow the lens angle to focus more directly on reflective practice as a process of professional development. The subject is formal professional development because, while reflective practice may take place in any situation, it is almost always learned in a formal learning setting of one kind or another—and our purpose in writing is to encourage the development and nurture of such learning opportunities. The first part of this chapter describes reflective practice as a professional development process: What does it look like? How does it begin? The second part of the chapter contrasts this mode of professional development with more traditional approaches focusing on differences in assumptions, content, and processes.

REFLECTIVE PRACTICE

Defining Reflective Practice

Reflective practice, while often confused with reflection, is neither a solitary nor a relaxed meditative process. To the contrary, reflective practice is a challenging, demanding, and often trying process that is most successful as a collaborative effort.

Although the term *reflective practice* is interpreted and understood in different ways,[1] within our discussion, reflective practice is viewed as a means by which practitioners can develop a greater level of self-awareness about the nature and impact of their performance, an awareness that creates opportunities for professional growth and development.

As explained in Chapter 1, awareness is essential for behavioral change. To gain a new level of insight into personal behavior, the reflective practitioner assumes a dual stance, being, on one hand, the actor in a drama and, on the other hand, the critic who sits in the audience watching and analyzing the entire performance. To achieve this perspective, individuals must come to an understanding of their own behavior; they must develop a conscious awareness of their own actions and effects and the ideas or theories-in-use that shape their action strategies.

Achieving this level of conscious awareness, however, is not an easy task. Theories-in-use, as we have seen, are not easily articulated. Schon (1983) has described this process in the context of professional practice. As he explained, professional knowledge is grounded in professional experience: "Competent practitioners usually know more than they can say. They exhibit a kind of knowing-in-practice, most of which is tacit" (p. viii). Consequently, when asked, master teachers or master administrators are often unable to identify the components of their work that lead to successful outcomes.[2] Similarly, practitioners who want to improve their performance are often unclear about how their own actions prevent them from being more successful. So, if the purpose of reflective practice is to enhance awareness of our own thoughts and action, as a means of professional growth, how do we begin this process of reflection? How do we begin to develop a critical awareness about our own professional practice? Where do we start?

Reflective Practice as Experiential Learning

Reflective practice is located within the older tradition of experiential learning and also the more recently defined perspective of situated cognition. Experiential learning theorists, including Dewey, Lewin, and Piaget, maintain that learning is most effective, most likely to lead to behavioral change, when it begins with experience, and specifically problematic experience. From experience and research, we know that learning is most effective when people become personally engaged in the learning process, and engagement is most likely to take place when there is a need to learn. In professional programs, for example, fruitful learning often doesn't begin until the person is on the job. Situated cognition focuses on both the process and the context of learning. In a view popularized by the recent attention to problem-based learning (Bridges, 1992), situated cognition proponents maintain that learning is best accomplished through an active, social, and authentic learning process. Learning, they argue, is most effective when the learner is actively involved in the learning process, when it takes place as a collaborative rather than an isolated activity, and when it takes place in a context relevant to the learner (Brown, Collins, & Duguid, 1989a, 1989b; Prestine & LeGrand, 1991).

Experiential learning theory maintains further that learning is a dialectic and cyclical process consisting of four stages: experience, observation and reflection, abstract reconceptualization, and experimentation (Kolb, 1984). While experience is the basis for learning, learning cannot take place without reflection. Conversely, while reflection is essential to the process, reflection must be integrally linked with action (Figure 2.1). Reflective practice, then, integrating theory and practice, thought and action, is, as Schon described, a "dialogue of thinking and doing through which I become more skillful" (1987, p. 31).

Figure 2.1. Experiential Learning Cycle

In this cyclical process, learning or the process of inquiry begins with what Dewey (1938b) described as a problematic or an indeterminate situation: a troublesome event or experience, an unsettling situation that cannot be resolved using standard operating procedures. Prompted by a sense of uncertainty or unease, the reflective practitioner steps back to examine this experience: What was the nature of the problem? What were my intentions? What did I do? What happened? In the process of observing and analyzing this experience, problems emerge. The problem—a discrepancy between the real and the ideal, between intention and action, or between action and effects—further stimulates the inquiry and motivates the learner to absorb new information as part of an active search for better answers and more effective strategies. The final stages of the process involve reconceptualization and experimentation. Having examined and analyzed the experience, the learner moves again into the realm of theory. Now motivated by an awareness of a problem, the learner uses new information to develop alternate theories that are more useful in explaining the relationship between actions and outcomes and to begin the search for strategies that are more consistent with espoused theories and more effective in achieving intended outcomes. This changed perspective becomes a stimulus for experimentation: New theories suggest different strategies that can then be tested through action. In short, raising questions about practice begins a learning process that leads to behavioral change. The section that follows illustrates each of these stages in more detail.

Concrete experience. Consistent with the model outlined above, the first step of the learning process is to identify problematic situations. Because the intent of reflective practice is to improve the quality of professional performance, we begin our inquiry by focusing on problems of practice.

There are many different types of problems (Getzels, 1979).[3] In some situations, the problem, with readily available solutions, is presented to the problem solver. In other situations, the problem emerges from one's own experience. In whatever form, problems arise out of a sense of discomfort or a desire to change. There is a discrepancy between what we perceive to be and what we consider desirable; in some way, the situation falls short of the ideal.

These discrepancies come to our attention in different ways. In some cases, information from another source—an individual or group or a report—helps us to see a problem. The space creature described in Chapter 1, for example, observes that, despite attempts at remediation, the pulled-out students continue to fall further behind and leads us to see a problem embedded in the daily schedule. Test scores demonstrating the progress (or its lack) among these students might serve the same purpose.

In other cases, our own experience helps us to identify problems. The new principal, for example, enthusiastically assumes the position only to find that, 6 months later, he or she is treated with mistrust by teachers. In this situation, a perceived discrepancy between intent and accomplishment creates a sense of a problem.

Dilemmas can also lead to problem identification. For example, in the course of making student assignments, an elementary school principal experienced being pulled between assigning each of a pair of twins to different rooms, the standard policy, and assigning them to the same room because of number imbalance and other issues.

Problem identification may also come through a surprise or attention to the unexpected. The same principal, a member of the district-wide administrative reflection group described in Chapter 7, once reported a surprising telephone call at a reflection meeting. She had been berated by a friend for her position on a proposed change in the reading curriculum. This call focused her attention and, when she introduced the issue in the administrative reflection group, led the entire group to a new level of understanding and awareness of a more complex set of problems. Particulars of this case are recounted in Chapter 7.

Regardless of how we develop awareness of the problem, its discovery or recognition motivates us to gather information of the sort the space creature possessed and moves us further into the reflection cycle. Acknowledgment of the twins' placement dilemma began an extended period of reflection about the children, the policy, and its educational and emotional effects on them and others. As a result, the principal altered the policy and assigned the twins together.

Not all problems are of equal dimensions. Problems that educators face, for example, come in all shapes and sizes. Some involve only a few people; others may involve an entire school. What is important, however, is not the scope or dimensions of the problem but the significance of the problem to the individual. In reflective practice, we are seeking deep engagement in learning, and relevance produces engagement: A relevant problem rivets attention and arouses the need to learn.

Identification of problems, however, is not easy. People, and educators in particular, desire to view things positively and to be optimistic. In response to organizational problems, discussion turns quickly to solutions while problem identification and analysis are cut short (Bolman & Deal, 1991). Identification of personal problems is even more difficult. Think of the child who comes to the parent with a problem but cannot bring herself to disclose it. Once the problem is spoken, what seemed overwhelming becomes manageable, but the resistance initially was great. Adults are not very different: Problems are often seen as an indicator of incompetence and failure. As a result, most of us have effective defenses for preventing problem recognition.

With practice in reflection, we learn to take a conscious orientation toward problem finding; but, initially, this step of the process may seem difficult or feel "unnatural." Although this skill develops quickly, because the learning cycle begins with problematic experience, one of the initial tasks of the facilitator in a formal reflective practice setting is to enable individuals to uncover or discover problematic situations within the context of their practice. Specific techniques are described in Chapters 3 and 4.

Observation and analysis. In the first stage of the process, the inquiry is focused on a particular aspect of practice. Finding the problem motivates the practitioner; there is a genuine need for new information. In the second stage of the process, the practitioner assumes the role of a researcher and begins to gather information. Because reflective practice focuses on personal behavior within the professional context, we begin to gather and analyze rich information about the experience and particularly about our own behavior. We become the critic watching our own actions on stage. We stand back from the experience itself, assume a more detached stance, and step outside the action to observe it critically and to describe it fully.

A full description incorporates cognitive and emotional aspects of behavior. Until now, we've focused primarily on cognition: examining espoused theories and theories-in-use. To understand experience, however, requires that we explore feelings that were aroused in the situation. Actions are influenced not only by ideas but by feelings as well; only by understanding the personal reactions of ourselves and others can we come to a full understanding of the problem and develop appropriate solutions. Consequently, when we gather information about experience, we mean the full range of human experience including beliefs, values, intentions, attitudes, feelings, ideas, and action (Osterman, 1990).

The means of obtaining observational data are broad and limited only by our own creativity. The purpose of the research inquiry is to further understanding in ways that will improve the craft performance. To meet that objective, we gather information in a wide variety of ways: self-reports and recollections, observations of our practice or simulated practice by others reported to us in various ways, completely objective data recorded on audio- or videotapes, documents such as memos, journals, minutes of meetings, or supervisory conference reports, feedback from survey research and action research projects, and sometimes information from debriefing of deliberately generated behaviors such as role plays. Much, if not most, of the data we collect in the observational phase will be qualitative rather than quantitative. The basic issues remain—usefulness, richness, and comprehensiveness.

Once information is at hand, we analyze the experience; we reflect upon it. Again, our goal is to achieve the detached perspective of the drama critic or the space creature. In the observational phase, our purpose was simply to describe the experience in a multidimensional and comprehensive way. Through reflection and analysis, we strive to understand the experience. Within the framework of the model presented in Chapter 1, we examine experience—both actions and outcomes—as a means to articulate and understand espoused theories and theories-in-use. Why did events take place as they did? What ideas or feelings prompted my actions? Did my actions correspond with my intentions? Did my actions lead to the outcomes I intended?

The term *reflection* is often thought of as a solitary and meditative process; and, in fact, analysis may be done alone—while listening to a tape recording of a committee meeting, watching ourself teach on a videotape, or analyzing the contents and attitudes contained in our memos. Nonetheless, because of the deeply ingrained nature of our behavioral patterns, it is sometimes difficult to develop a critical perspective on our own behavior. For that reason alone, analysis occurring in a collaborative and cooperative environment is likely to lead to greater learning. The whole committee might analyze the tape recording; you and a supervisor might probe into the teaching episode together; a colleague who has "shadowed" you all day might help to analyze what he or she saw.

The process of inquiry began with a problematic or indeterminate situation. In the initial stages, understanding of the problem may have been little more than an intuitive sense or a gut feeling that something was wrong or could be better. Through these integrally linked processes of observation and analysis, we come to see clearly the discrepancies, incongruities, and failures to reach intentions. The problem begins to emerge more clearly, and we begin to see our own role in the problem more clearly.

An example from the administrative reflection group illustrates how reflective analysis affects the formulation of the problem and leads to even deeper reflection. The superintendent described his concern about essays a group of high school seniors had written after returning from several weeks as exchange students in Moscow. As he explained, the essays lacked feeling. They followed the essay form but communicated little meaning. Over the next few months, the group analyzed this problem and from their discussion emerged a much broader concern about the orientation of secondary teachers as "dispensers of knowledge." At this point, the problem had shifted. The issue was no longer the quality of student essays but a pervasive instructional orientation that does not foster the learning outcomes that they envision. This understanding led them to formulate a new problem: How do we as district leaders work to transform an instructional orientation we believe does not result in the best possible education? This reframing also motivated them to search for their own metaphor for secondary teaching and provided an ongoing focus for group reflection.

Argyris and Schon (1974) made a distinction between single-loop learning and double-loop learning. The "fix-it" model is a form of single-loop learning: A solution is developed to correct the presenting problem, but the underlying causes of the problem are neither recognized nor addressed. Single-loop learning is largely ineffective in contributing to long-term solutions to problems because the underlying assumptions that reinforce the ineffective behaviors are never examined. Double-loop learning, on the other hand, holds the potential for real change because it examines these underlying assumptions, or theories-in-use, as part of the problem-solving process. Analysis within the framework of reflective practice is designed to lead to double-loop learning. At the completion of this phase, the practitioner has come to an understanding—incomplete though it may be—of espoused theories and theories-in-use. With this knowledge in hand, the practitioner begins the next stage of inquiry: reconceptualization.

Abstract reconceptualization. In the third stage of the learning cycle, we consider alternate ways of thinking and acting. We consider new action theories that encompass the relationship between actions and outcomes. At this point in the conceptual framework outlined in Chapter 1, the practitioner has identified a problem or problem area and, through observation and reflection, has come to understand what was done and why. This theory-in-use, now articulated, has been examined relative to the espoused theory and assessed for effectiveness. With this complete behavioral description in place, the practitioner is now ready to reconsider old ideas and to search for new ones that will lead to a greater alignment between ideas, actions, and outcomes.

This point in the cycle involves an active search for new ideas and new strategies. We are highly motivated to find new information, theories, techniques, or processes to address *our* problem. At this point, we know what we did in the prior situation, and we have an idea of why we did it. We are also well aware of why it didn't work. The objective now is to develop alternate hypotheses or action research strategies that may address the problem. To do that, we gather information that will help us to develop a more effective conceptual and strategic approach.

At every stage of the cycle, the nature of the learning has been personal and engaging. The problem is self-defined and relevant, and the process of observation and analysis in focusing on the individual role in the problem context generates a felt need to improve, change, or reinforce effective behaviors. At this stage of reconceptualization, then, the professional is strongly motivated to seek out and consider new ideas.

We are prompted to try things that before we rejected. We see relevance in ideas that formerly seemed irrelevant. We are now able to make connections between theory and practice, to integrate new information and ideas into our practice. We are now beginning to reshape theories-in-use.

Unlike traditional models of professional development, in the reflective practice approach, the practitioner can use information from a wide variety of sources from the worlds of research and practice. The important issue again is not the source but its utility. As Chapter 6 illustrates, practitioners may find relevant information in research studies or other publications and workshops or formal study. Observations or discussions with colleagues may serve a similar purpose. Confronted with the problem and now with a clearer understanding of the problem and our own role in that problem, the search for knowledge becomes more directed and focused, and—an important distinction—the search is self-directed.

There are many ways to approach the reconceptualization stage. We may do it alone through reading or finding already existing "answers." We may take a more creative self-definitional approach. And we may find great value in working collaboratively with others also attempting to work through solutions to the same or similar problems (Miller, 1990a). In working with colleagues, we greatly increase the pool of available ideas and resources. As one participant in a reflection group said: "I have available to me many lives that I have not lived."

Active experimentation. The final stage in experiential learning is testing our reconceptualized behavior and assumptions. In the reconceptualization phase, we developed new action theories and framed them as hypotheses. With regard to collaborative decision making, for example, one might focus on the hypothesis that, by giving away control, we gain control. We have articulated an action theory that maintains that, if we act in a particular way, we can expect a particular type of response. In this stage of the cycle, we begin to test this assumption. We make a conscious decision to act in a particular way to test this new conceptualization: We engage in behavioral experiments. These may be trials of our new ideas in actual workplaces or they may be role plays in the relative safety of a reflection group.

This stage completes one cycle and begins another. The experiment produces new concrete experience and the learning process begins anew, but with one important difference. By now, our reflective skills have developed and self-awareness is acute and focused. Although, in the early experiences with reflective practice, it was difficult to distance ourselves from our performance, at this stage of experimentation we go into the action better able to handle the dual role of actor and drama critic. We ourselves are more skilled at gathering information: We are more aware of our own actions, more sensitive to the feelings and reactions of others, and more adept at using a variety of techniques to gather information. At this point, the circular nature of the process is obvious. With the data in hand, we analyze the sequence of events to confirm or disconfirm the new hypothesis. Confirmation reinforces the new theory and provides an incentive for repeating what initially may have been awkward behaviors. Those instances where the experiment doesn't work as expected lead to a renewed search to refine the theory and/or to develop strategies that are more appropriate tests of the theory. Whether the next cycle focuses in a more detailed way on the same problem or addresses another issue, it builds upon and profits from the earlier cycle: Learning and professional development become a progressive and continuing process.

Experiential Learning in Action

We have described reflective practice as a form of experiential learning and have done so in a linear and segmented fashion. This was done for conceptual clarity but does not adequately describe the process itself, which is far more fluid and holistic. As the narratives in Chapters 5, 6, and 7 illustrate, when we engage in reflective practice, we move back and forth among the stages. For example, some new idea in the reconceptualization stage may momentarily take us back to the analysis phase to check out something we did not think about earlier. Often we will not be aware of particular "stages" in our reflection. In other instances, dialogue might show evidence that several stages were brought into play almost simultaneously. This will occur even more often when we become very adept at reflection, for reflection like other activities becomes habitual. For newcomers to the reflective process, whether as participants or facilitators, however, it is probably good counsel to keep the four stages of the experiential cycle clearly in mind as road signs to guide learning and progress through the process.

CONTRASTING TRADITIONAL AND REFLECTIVE APPROACHES TO PROFESSIONAL DEVELOPMENT

Professional development processes share a common goal: improved practice. Nonetheless, there are distinctly different strategies or routes toward that goal. Reflective practice is a professional development process that we believe is highly effective in achieving behavioral change. We also maintain that reflective practice and its underlying assumptions are in sharp contrast with the traditional practice of professional development. So, while our purpose in writing is to encourage the use of reflective practice for professional development, we feel that the arguments about change developed in Chapter 1 are relevant here. Before we can adopt new behaviors, before we can begin to introduce reflective practice as a professional development strategy whether in a university classroom, a school, or a school district, it is necessary (a) that we develop an awareness of our habitual actions and the assumptions that shape those actions and (b) that we consider the effectiveness of actions relative to intentions.

As a means of heightening awareness, the following section describes two contrasting routes to professional development and compares their purposes, assumptions, and practices.

Traditional Professional Development: A Portrait

If we observed a typical professional development session in a university classroom, a school district, a principal or teacher center, or a corporate headquarters, we would likely see this scene: The instructor, often an outside expert, is clearly identifiable. He or she usually occupies a central position at the front of the room and is accompanied by handouts and visual aids. The presentation usually focuses on a single concept, program, or model that, if implemented, will lead to positive change. Although some presentations provide a longer period of time (perhaps a week), the majority of professional development sessions range from a few hours to a day. For the session, the instructor has a carefully outlined plan intended to convey information to the learners. Although the learners may have an opportunity to ask questions and experiment with the new skills, for the most part, they sit facing the instructor and listen. Questions tend to be infrequent, and presentations are seldom interrupted. Although ostensibly geared to "success" in the professional context, professional education consists primarily of transmission of knowledge. In this process, knowledge is the province of experts, and learners have access to it through the instructor. The instructor's role is to convey that information in a clear and concise manner; the learner's role is to absorb it.

Reflective Professional Development: A Portrait

If we walk into a reflectively based professional development session in a university classroom, a school district, or a principal development center, we are, by contrast, less likely to be able to predict the scene. We might see pairs of individuals, or groups of four to six or more, engaged in discussion. We might observe a role play in action or a number of them going on simultaneously. We might find someone providing information while others in the room listen. We might find everyone writing for periods of up to 5 to 7 minutes. Most likely, we will find participants seated in circles or around tables—but not in rows facing a single point. In many cases, we would not be able to recognize the instructor instantly and, when we do, we will notice that he or she plays a very different role. He or she might be at the front of the room providing information, but it is just as likely that he or she will be seated with others participating in a discussion doing more listening than talking. She or he might even be out of the room while participants engage in cooperative learning activities and carry on animated, focused interaction with each other.

While the particular activity occurring in a reflectively based development session is more difficult to predict than in a traditionally based session, there are expected behavioral regularities. Students are active participants in the learning process, helping to establish the agenda and shaping the learning process to meet their own needs. The nature of the discussion is as likely to focus on emotions as on ideas and the ideas discussed are those gathered from personal experience as well as from reading and research. Information is provided by all participants. Multiple centers of activity often occur simultaneously. Many questions are placed by different individuals and answers are as likely to come from other participants as from the instructor.

From these brief descriptions, it's possible to see that, while the two approaches may have the same goal, their immediate objectives or purpose are different. It is also apparent that very different assumptions about the nature of learning operate in each setting and that these theories-in-use influence both content and process.

Purpose. The ultimate purpose in the traditional model may be improved performance, but the directly observable purpose—and the purpose embedded in the theory-in-use guiding the behaviors of both instructor and participants—clearly is knowledge acquisition. The instructor spends most of the available time in these sessions transferring information to generally passive recipients and testing the acquisition of that information.

The immediate as well as ultimate purpose of reflective professional development is not knowledge acquisition per se but behavioral change and improved performance. This is readily observable in development sessions. Attention is focused directly on behavior, either behavior enacted before the session and recollected and analyzed during the meeting or behavior generated during the session itself. While at various times the facilitator may provide information or theories, such presentations are focused directly on behavior change and improvement of performance.

Assumptions. From these observations, we infer that the two models differ greatly in their assumptions about behavioral change. In the traditional model, most of the time is consumed in giving and receiving public knowledge, knowledge that is available to all and that is not personal or based on individual experience. The primary assumption is that acquisition of shared knowledge will lead to behavioral change. Theory, thoroughly understood and carefully applied, means good practice. The traditional approach to professional development, then, reflects an underlying assumption that information is a stimulus for behavioral change, that individuals receiving knowledge will use it to improve performance. Knowing a better way to behave, individuals will simply act on the knowledge. This approach places total faith in rational processes as the source of behavior. In the terms of Chapter 1, it focuses exclusively on changing espoused theory with the belief that, when intentions change, behavior will also change. This is a very simple theory of behavioral change. It is tenaciously held both in general education and in professional development—but the results typically do not match the faith put in it.

In reality, there is little evidence that this approach works well and more reason to believe that it seldom leads to noticeable improvement or change in professional practice. In-service programs in schools and school districts, for example, typically employ research, development, and diffusion (RD&D) models or what House (1981) termed a *technological perspective* and Bennis, Benne, and Chin (1961) called a *rational-empirical approach*. In this orientation, "experts" come into a district for a day or longer and present a program that is designed to bring a successful change: improved instruction, higher self-esteem, more effective problem solving, better student discipline. Despite the quality of the presentation and the validity of the model being presented, the evidence is not strong that this method leads to significant, long-lasting, or widespread change in practice (Firestone & Corbett, 1988; Sarason, 1971, 1990). Teachers often return to classrooms enthused and excited about the possibility of reaching their students in more meaningful ways, but, despite the best intentions, fall back into the same patterns. Similarly, the administrator introduced to more effective methods of supervision and evaluation finds that day-to-day pressures and demands make it impossible to try the suggested alternatives. The status quo maintains itself. The more things change, the more they stay the same. The new information or program doesn't produce the desired results. But, next year, another attempt at change is made. The assumption remains the same: New information will lead to change. If the change doesn't occur, the fault is with the specific idea or with the professional to whom the idea has been presented.

The assumptions made about behavioral change in the reflective practice model are more complex than in the traditional model of professional development. They include the propositions about change described in Chapter 1. Behavioral change comes through self-awareness of formerly unrecognized assumptions lying in the theory-in-use, unrecognized habitual behaviors, and unrecognized negative outcomes of these behaviors. Change is a process begun not by learning a new idea from an expert but by recognition that something is not exactly "right" in one's own professional practice. It is initiated not through a standard set of information received in a large group but through careful attention to individual practice. The motivating force behind change is not the goodness or usefulness of an idea from an external source but the desire to function well in a professional capacity coupled with the awareness that current behavior is not fully reaching this goal.

In reflective practice, change includes an emotional as well as a rational dimension. Because behavioral change is personal change, it entails emotions. Emotions attach to the ways we view ourselves, our actions, and their results. When we inquire into our own unrecognized assumptions and behaviors and find them wanting, there is an emotional load associated with self-confrontation and with personal wrestling about how to respond to the awareness. On the other hand, when we inquire into our own unrecognized assumptions and find them to be positive and effective, there is a strong positive emotional response. Reflective practice assumes the centrality of emotion along with cognition. It strives to recognize, work with, and support the emotional aspect of behavioral change.

That personal behavioral change always intersects with culture is another assumption undergirding reflective practice. Unrecognized, habitual behaviors result from deep acculturation. Behavioral change, then, entails changing the relationship between culture and behavior. Often, behavioral changes resulting from successful reflection are at odds with the ongoing larger and organizational culture. This means that individuals undergoing personal change will likely be somewhat more at odds with the norms and assumptions of the culture than before. Thus reflective practice assumes that achieving and maintaining desired personal changes also means working for cultural changes, ones that will then buttress the new behaviors. Understanding the cultural dimension of change helps us see why the "fix-it" approach of the traditional model so frequently fails. The "fix-it" orientation replaces a part or piece assumed to be broken, but it pays no heed to the culture in which the part is embedded or to the relationship between the cultural values and assumptions and those residing in the part. When the "fix" is not supported by the surrounding culture, it is quickly rejected. This is especially true when the relationship between behavior and culture remains unrecognized.

In the way that action theories shape behavior, these assumptions about learning, and specifically professional development, directly shape the method of instruction that is adopted: both content and process.

Content. The knowledge bases for traditional and reflective practice approaches to professional development also differ. As already noted, the traditional approach emphasizes knowledge transmission as the means toward improved practice. This knowledge may be described as public knowledge, knowledge as given, and knowledge as content. Public knowledge is "information, skills, perspectives, facts, ways of knowing . . . valued because it is accepted within the traditions of knowledge . . . it has received some degree of acceptance using 'public principles that stand as impersonal standards' . . . traditions of knowledge that have stood the test of time" (Berlak & Berlak, 1981, p. 145). Knowledge is given when it is assumed to be "a truth 'out there' " (p. 148), knowledge that has been discovered and verified. It can then be "given" or transmitted to others. Knowledge as content is a form of public knowledge that has been organized as "bodies of information, codified facts, theories, [and] generalizations" (p. 147).

The kind of knowledge transmitted in traditional approaches, especially graduate courses, is often called "theory," or what Schon described as a knowledge that is "specialized, firmly bounded, scientific, and standardized" (1983, p. 23). Those who assume such knowledge will improve practice also assume that what is "wrong" with practice or "needs improvement" is relatively generalized or standard across individuals and that it is best assessed and prescribed from an external, objective position by experts possessing theoretical knowledge.

In the traditional model, practice assumes a secondary, subordinate relationship to public, given, or theoretical knowledge. The link between theory and practice is implicit, and the learning process begins and ends with theory or public knowledge. The central question is this: "What do others—experts, researchers, developers of theoretical knowledge—'know' that they think others *should* know?" Theory and practice remain separate, distinct, and unequal. "Theory" courses are taught by academicians and workshops are delivered by experts. Both can be described as a struggle to penetrate the meaning of abstractions about organizational realities framed in abstract terms that make connections to concrete realities implausible. Even so-called practice courses, taught by practitioners—often retired administrators—containing mostly "war stories," are really based on many of the same assumptions as "theory" courses. In these cases, an individual takes his or her own experience and "elevates" it to the status of given, public knowledge and generalizes it to the needs of others without the support of the verifying mechanisms used in developing theoretical knowledge. What remains the same in both "theory" and "practice" traditional approaches is an external agent who decides what the participants need and transmits it to them. In either case, the knowledge possessed by the instructor is more important than that possessed by the learner and in neither case is direct attention paid to the individual practice of the learner.

The knowledge bases employed in the reflective practice approach to professional development are more varied and complex than those in the traditional approach. Whereas in the traditional model of professional development, public, content, and given knowledge are both the beginning and the end of the process, in the reflective model, this kind of knowledge is used in more limited ways. Transmission of such knowledge is useful in consciousness- or awareness-raising as a stimulus to thinking about discrepancies between intentions and actions or espoused theories and theories-in-use. It is also useful as a source of possibilities for new ways of behaving *after* discrepancies are acknowledged and the individual is motivated to change.

In reflective practice, other varieties of knowledge are central. These are described as personal knowledge, knowledge as problematic, and knowledge as process. A personal knowledge perspective assumes that "worthwhileness . . . cannot be judged apart from its relationship to the knower. Knowledge is useful only in so far [*sic*] as it enables persons to make sense of experience. [It] is gained from the 'inside.' [It] has the connotation of *Verstehen* or holistic understanding" (Berlak & Berlak, 1981, p. 145). As opposed to given knowledge, assuming knowledge is problematic treats it as "constructed, provisional, tentative" (p. 148). This means taking a creative, critical, and analytical orientation. Whereas treating knowledge as content emphasizes a codified body, treating knowledge as process emphasizes the "thinking, reasoning, and testing used to establish the truth or adequacy of a body of content" (p. 147).

While these are technical descriptors of the knowledge used in reflective practice, the central issue is that in reflection the predominant, but not sole, emphasis is on knowledge about personal professional practice. Underlying the reflective process is the assumption that useful knowledge addresses specific needs of the individual or constituency; it is experiential knowledge, practitioner knowledge, knowledge of craft, knowledge of personal action theories, and what Schon (1983) called knowing-in-action. Professional growth is envisioned as an odyssey whose purpose is not knowledge in an abstract sense but knowledge of a very personal and purposeful nature. Because the primary purpose in reflective practice is improved performance, the learning process begins with examining practice, and formal education becomes a laboratory for developing improved practice. In this laboratory, the typical relationship between theory and practice is inverted. In the traditional model, theory or public knowledge is the means to improve practice; in the reflective model, attention to practice is the means toward the development and refinement of theory—specifically, personal action theory. Within the reflective process, study of formal theory functions as an important resource in the developmental process, but it is not an end in itself.

In the reflective practice model, the link between theory and practice is explicit—not implicit as in the traditional approach—and the developmental process begins with practice. If we wish to develop new and better methods of practice, we begin by examining the behavior we want to improve. The central knowledge questions are much broader than in the traditional approach: "What do we do, and why do we do it?" "How do our knowledge, our understanding, our personal theoretical framework affect our own behavior?" "Given new knowledge, what will we do differently?" In the reflective approach, several kinds of knowledge are integrated. Theory *and* practice are integral and central considerations, and theory includes ideas derived both from formal research and from personal experience. Attention to public knowledge and formal theory is not lost or diminished, but practice—specifically, personal practice—assumes a far greater importance.

Process. Instructional strategies also differ between the two modes of professional development. Because of the central (but we believe faulty) assumption that knowledge transmission leads to behavioral change and the corresponding belief that knowledge is developed and interpreted by researchers or academicians rather than by practitioners, didacticism is the central and legitimate means in the traditional model. Although various strategies may be used—lecture, discussion, case study analysis—the central purpose remains to convey knowledge and to develop cognitive skills. Reflective practice, in contrast, relies to a greater extent on dialectic learning and, as we have seen, is rooted in the experience—and particularly the problematic experience—of the learners.

Given the emphasis on public, given, and content knowledge, the instructor assumes the dominant role in the process while the learner functions in a subordinate, largely passive role. In reflective practice, the shift in focus and purpose of learning alters the nature of the learner-instructor relationship and shifts the balance of power and control. In the traditional model, power—to define problems, develop knowledge, prescribe answers, determine processes—and hence control over the nature, direction, and outcomes, rests with organizational superiors: university professors, consultants, or other external experts. Participants in professional development are essentially controlled by others. In juxtaposition, power and control in the reflective process are shared.

In the traditional model, the practitioner adopts a passive role as a consumer of knowledge. In the reflective practice model, the learner's role is far more active: "The practitioner becomes a researcher . . . and engages in a continuing process of self-education" (Schon, 1983, p. 299). In doing so, the learner assumes a central position, and the model of instructor as expert gives way to that of the instructor as facilitator. The role of the leader is no longer to deliver but to guide—to provide information and resources to facilitate the individual's personal inquiry and professional growth. The facilitator enters into what Schon (1983) called a *reflective conversation*. In this relationship, the instructor is not an expert responsible for conveying standardized and scientifically determined knowledge to guide the actions of the practitioner but a communication specialist engaged in a discussion of personal meaning. In Dewey's words, the educator can no longer "start with knowledge already organized and proceed to ladle it out in doses" (1938a, p. 82).

In the traditional model, the learner clearly is a subordinate. The instructor establishes expectations and provides the expertise; the learner complies with these expectations and comprehends what is offered. In the reflective practice model, this instructor-learner relationship changes. Responsibility for the success of the learning endeavor belongs no longer to either the learner or the facilitator but is shared by both. The learner is active and directive in the learning process, and the facilitator and learner—each of whom brings knowledge and expertise to the situation—become collaborators working on a shared task.

There are three other aspects of the learning process that contrast with the development modes. In the traditional approach, learning is molecular, while, in the reflective approach, it is holistic. The "fix-it" orientation of traditional development often focuses on discrete skills or segments of behavior and organizational life. Reflective practice assumes a holistic approach to learning. Beginning with individual behavior, anything related to it becomes part of the process. At the very least, this includes the individual's background and cultural context. In the traditional situation, with its emphasis on knowledge transmission, the primary emphasis is on cognition, but only in a very narrowly defined sense. The learner, as a student, is expected to gather and retain information that can be applied to problems of practice; in that sense, there is little need to involve the individual as a person. In reflective practice, however, the intent is to enable the individual to develop competence. Accordingly, the focus expands to incorporate the individual as person. Individuals are assumed to have cognitive, emotional, and social dimensions. Learning to behave in different ways involves all of these. The concept of cognition also expands from a narrow emphasis on information gathering or recall to the development of analytic and conceptual skills that enable the individual to create knowledge needed to respond to the diverse demands of practice. Finally, in the reflective mode, learning is a social process, whereas, in the traditional mode, it is individual. In the usual process, learners are addressed as isolated individuals learning in parallel but not interrelated ways. In reflective practice, learning is cooperatively based. Collaboration extends beyond the learner-facilitator relationship to include all of the individuals in an interdependent learning process.

Table 2.1 presents a condensed summary of the various contrasting assumptional and belief differences for the traditional and reflective practice models of professional development.

SUMMARY

At this point, we have completed the conceptual framework to prepare us to engage in reflective practice. Chapter 1 provided the broad explanation of behavioral and organizational stability and change. In this chapter, we detailed a four-stage experiential learning cycle that is the heart of the reflective process. We also looked more specifically at the assumptions underlying reflective practice as a mode of professional development (and contrasted these with the familiar traditional mode). With this conceptual framework in place, the next two chapters are much more "how-to" oriented. The first details the assumptions and skills needed to facilitate reflective professional development. The second details various means we have found useful for moving individuals and groups through various stages of the experiential learning cycle.

TABLE 2.1

Contrasting Approaches to Professional Development

	Traditional Model	Reflective Practice Model
PURPOSE	Knowledge acquisition	Behavioral change
ASSUMPTIONS	Change via standardized knowledge	Change via self-awareness
CONTENT	Change: Rational	Change: Rational, emotional, social, cultural
	Knowledge:	Knowledge:
	Public	Public & personal
	Given	Given & problematic
	Content	Content & process
	Theory:	Theory *and* practice
	Espoused theory	Behavior: Espoused & theories-in-use, actions & outcomes
PROCESS	Theory/practice: Implicit/discrete	Theory/practice: Explicit/integral
	Didactic/abstract	Dialectic/Experimental
	Individual, molecular, cognitive	Collaborative, holistic, personal
	Instructor as expert	Instructor as facilitator
	Learner as subordinate	Learner as agent
	Practitioner as passive consumer	Practitioner as action researcher

41

NOTES

1. Grimmett and Erickson (1988), for example, identify three different ways of describing reflection: (a) as thoughtfulness about action, (b) as deliberation and choice among competing versions of good practice, and (c) as reconstructing experience, the end of which is the identification of a new possibility for action.

2. Preparation programs always have student teaching or administrative internships fulfilling the practice component of learning. As we argue, however, some very masterful professionals are unable to explain the underlying principles or theories-in-use that guide their practice. If this is the case, the student must either extrapolate the underlying principles for him- or herself or else treat the masterful performance as discrete actions to be copied without consideration of contextual factors. Reflective practice may be powerfully applied to internship experiences as a learning vehicle for both the novice and more experienced practitioners. We do not provide a specific "story" of such use of reflection, though, at Hofstra, our curriculum, including internship activities, is being organized around reflective principles. Barnett (1990) has described reflection in internship situations in detail.

3. Technically, a *problem* is conceptually different than the *problematic situation* in terms of clarity and specificity; however, the terms are used synonymously here with the understanding that, through the process of reflection, the nature and understanding of the problem may change dramatically.

3 How to Nurture Reflection

Reflective practice, like an orchid, requires special conditions to thrive. One of the most important elements in the environment is trust. In this chapter, we discuss some of the factors that nurture trust and create an environment conducive to reflective practice, with particular attention to the facilitator's role.

THE CONTEXT FOR REFLECTION

Reflective practice can take place almost anywhere. An assistant superintendent for personnel sets aside an hour to review her efforts to recruit minority staff for the district in an effort to develop a more effective approach. Two teachers meet in the hall or lunchroom and begin to talk about a situation that occurred that morning in one of their classrooms. A principal stops by the office of the new assistant principal and asks how the job has been going. A superintendent meets on an ongoing basis with a team of administrators and university faculty members to discuss educational leadership. A group of principals gather for a weekly work session as part of a staff development program. Several teachers meet as part of their efforts to improve the quality of the reading program. An intern meets with his or her supervisor to discuss the week's experiences. Reflective practice can take place on an informal basis occurring in the course of daily activities. It can be an integral part of the postobservation supervisory conference; it can provide the framework of a professional development program offered in a university, school, or district. In other words, reflective practice can take place on a formal or informal basis anytime one or more persons begin a process of inquiry for the purpose of examining actions and events as a means to understand and improve performance.

Reflective practice *can* take place anywhere, but, to thrive, it requires a nurturing environment, an environment characterized by openness and trust. Some of the situations described above are not typical. In schools and other organizations as well, it's not uncommon to find two colleagues working together: New teachers connect with other new teachers to share their woes and joys; two principals —usually not from the same district—swap shoptalk on an occasional basis. It is uncommon, however, to find groups of teachers or administrators from the same district meeting to talk about individual and mutual problems. Even less likely is finding teams or collegial efforts that cross hierarchical lines: teachers meeting with administrators, building principals and central office administrators meeting with one another and with the superintendent (Cohn & Lenz, 1990). In schools and school districts, as in other organizations, we seldom discuss our professional problems with superiors or with subordinates, and we seldom share problems with our peers for fear that it may affect opportunities for tenure or promotion.

Reflective practice in a group setting is a high risk process. It requires an openness that goes against the grain in most organizational situations (Argyris, 1990). In most organizations, problems are viewed as a sign of weakness. The teacher who has discipline problems in the classroom doesn't ask for advice or assistance because, by admitting he has problems, he believes he's admitting to incompetence. The administrator who is unsuccessful in implementing site-based management continues to use the same ineffective strategies because she's afraid to admit that she's not succeeding. To break this conspiracy of silence requires new organizational norms. To engage in the reflective process, individuals need to believe that discussion of problems will not be interpreted as incompetence or weakness. No one will talk about problems—personal or organizational—unless they feel safe, secure, and able to take a risk. In essence, engaging in reflective practice requires trust. If the assistant principal didn't trust the principal, it's unlikely that his question would yield anything more informative or productive than this type of statement: "Fine, thanks, no problems." If the teachers did not trust one another and their administrator, it's unlikely that they would admit to having problems and begin to discuss those problems as a means toward developing more effective strategies. Where reflective practice occurs, people are willing to share sensitive information about their performance with their colleagues and discuss those areas of their practice where they may be weak or at least not as strong as they would like.

Trust is perhaps the essential condition needed to foster reflective practice in any environment. If the reflective process is going to flourish in an organizational setting, the participants must be confident that the information they disclose will not be used against them —in subtle or not so subtle ways. The development of a climate of trust in any setting requires intentional action and intervention; someone must act as a buffer to protect confidences and to provide safety. In an organizational setting, this sense of security often requires the authorization of a superior: Subordinates will not speak freely unless the superior clearly and convincingly demonstrates that speaking freely is acceptable and will not lead to unpleasant consequences. These same norms of safety also must be firmly established within the group itself: Individuals must trust one another to maintain confidentiality.

Reflective practice requires a facilitator, someone who helps to begin the process and assumes responsibility for ensuring the participants' safety. In some cases, the facilitator can be the same person who serves as the organizational buffer: a teacher working with the aides in her room, a principal working with a group of teachers, the superintendent working with principals and teachers. In other cases, the facilitator may be a university faculty member or a consultant brought into the district.

Because trust is an essential ingredient in the process of reflective practice, one of the first responsibilities of the facilitator is to build trust. But how does that happen? There are several techniques that are effective in establishing trust and facilitating reflective practice, but by now it should be clear that actions are directly influenced by underlying assumptions and beliefs (theories-in-use). Consequently, in the following section, we outline first some key beliefs (theories-in-use) that seem essential to reflective practice and, second, communication techniques (strategies) that facilitate reflective practice. These beliefs and strategies influence reflective practice in two ways. First, they engender trust, which is a basic precondition for reflective practice. Second, they are the material and the method for reflective practice. The issues are ideas that will inevitably emerge in discussions of professional practice; the communication methods are, by their very nature, means to reflection.

Because the facilitator's interaction with the group is critical in determining whether and to what extent trust develops and grows among the members of the reflective group, these beliefs and methods are an important part of the facilitator's conceptual framework and repertoire of skills.

KEY ASSUMPTIONS

To serve as an effective facilitator, actions have to be grounded in a certain set of beliefs, beliefs that reflect a deep commitment to the potential for human change and development. These beliefs about professional development constitute a "credo for reflective practice."

Credo for Reflective Practice

1. Everyone needs professional growth opportunities.
2. All professionals want to improve.
3. All professionals *can* learn.

4. All professionals are capable of assuming responsibility for their own professional growth and development.
5. People need and want information about their own performance.
6. Collaboration enriches professional development.

The facilitator in the reflective process must be someone who strongly accepts these beliefs about professional development. We know a great deal about the importance of expectations. If teachers have high expectations for students, students learn. If principals have high expectations for staff, staff members rise to the occasion and lead the school to high levels of success. To communicate high expectations requires more than speeches and awards assemblies, it depends on deeply rooted beliefs that, if given the opportunity, individuals can actually meet high expectations. An interesting experimental study illustrates this point.

In the first phase of this study, teachers were videotaped while they talked for several minutes about two students from their classrooms, one a good student and the other a weak student. In the second phase, the two students described by the teachers were called into the classroom and were taught by the same teacher for 2-5 minutes. In both situations, the video- and audiotapes captured facial expressions, body language, and speech. At a later point, a group of fourth graders (along with groups of older students and adults) were asked to view 10-second clips from the tapes and to rate the academic ability of the students and the feelings of the teachers toward the students. Although the teachers tried to disguise their feelings, the study showed that even young students could easily detect the level of student performance and the extent to which the teacher loved the student (Babad, Bernieri, & Rosenthal, 1991).

In other words, true feelings are conveyed in very subtle ways that are difficult to disguise. Unless the facilitator has a deep commitment to these beliefs about professional development—or at least can suspend doubt—she or he will be unable to disguise real feelings. The facilitator has to be a person who not only espouses this educational philosophy but who can convince others through deeds that he or she can be trusted to fulfill the obligation.

Although these beliefs may seem obvious, as the following discussion of the individual principles suggests, they may not be as widely held as we might imagine.

(1) Everyone needs professional growth opportunities. The effective facilitator should accept that professional growth is a normal and necessary part of life for all members of the organization. This belief that *all* professionals need improvement is also closely linked to the understanding that all professionals experience situations in which they are not as competent as they would like, that all professionals confront problems in their daily work that require new and different strategies.

Problems of professional practice are the norm rather than the exception and there are few persons who don't experience difficulties in the work setting, but the "system" conveys a very different set of signals about problems and the people who admit to them. Teachers who have difficulties with student behavior are deemed deficient in classroom management, particularly if they attempt to refer these students to the principal. Administrators who are unable to contain parent complaints or minimize teacher grievances are viewed as incompetent by the central office. Even though the educational system by its very nature constantly generates new and changing problems and even though teaching and administration should be viewed as problem-solving occupations, problems are viewed as the exception rather than the norm and as a sign of incompetence rather than the everyday reality of organizational life. In other words, professional development is not necessarily viewed as a normal and ongoing professional need.

(2) All professionals want to improve. Reflective practice is based on the assumption that all professionals *want* professional growth opportunities. Some motivational theorists (Connell & Wellborn, 1989; deCharms, 1968, 1976, 1984; Deci & Ryan, 1985) view competence as a basic psychological need: Individuals need to experience themselves as capable of producing desired outcomes and avoiding negative outcomes. They need to experience themselves as effective professionals. This means that teachers who are unable to reach "at-risk"

students and administrators who are unable to maintain a safe, secure, and clean environment will have a strong desire to improve the quality of their performance. Any opportunity for them to develop their expertise and their competence will have a positive motivational effect.

This belief is not evident within the school community. To the contrary, we seem to assume that educators, whether teachers or administrators, avoid staff development and resist change. For example, think of the strategies designed to ensure that teachers attend all-day faculty conferences: from attendance sheets to memos to the file, threats, and fiscal penalties. If it were assumed that teachers wanted professional growth, there would be no reason to develop elaborate control mechanisms to ensure attendance. Although research and experience demonstrate that change in professional practice is, in fact, hard to achieve, there is some evidence to suggest that this resistance to change is rooted in organizational policy and practice rather than in a lack of intrinsic motivation. A student in a personnel management course, for example, interviewed the department chair and teachers in a special education department about professional growth. The teachers reported that they felt incompetent to handle the wide range of student needs that they confronted and that they desperately needed and wanted more information. The department chair, on the other hand, reported that the teachers had no interest in the scheduled staff development programs (none of which addressed the expressed needs of the teachers) and incorrectly concluded that the staff were not motivated to improve.

Reflective practice is based on an assumption that professional growth is as important to the individual as it is to the organization. While staff development may be designed with the needs of the organization in mind, reflective practice is a bottom-up approach prompted by the belief that organizational needs are best met by meeting the professionally oriented needs of individuals.

(3) All professionals can learn. This is probably one of the most difficult facets of the reflective practice credo. Despite what we say, there are few educators who truly believe that persons whose performance is deemed to be incompetent or marginal can improve,

particularly when the professional is a "seasoned" teacher or admin-istrator. In contrast, the prevailing theory-in-use is illustrated when we talk about people being "set in their ways" and conclude that "you can't teach an old dog new tricks." Our espoused theories are chal-lenged when we confront someone whose performance is poor or marginally acceptable regardless of age or experience, and our pes-simism regarding the possibility of change is likely to increase as individuals progress in age and experience.

(4) All professionals are capable of assuming responsibility for their own professional growth and development. The process of re-flective practice requires that the instructor give up the role of expert and adopt a new role as facilitator (see Chapter 2). This is not a simple task. If we examine our communication, we find that many of our habitual speech patterns have the unintended effect of blocking com-munication. While it may not be surprising to find that ordering, directing, commanding, warning, admonishing, and threatening are obstacles to communication, it may be surprising that apparently innocuous communication strategies such as moralizing, preaching, advising, suggesting, solving, persuading with logic, and even con-soling and praising can have the same negative effect on interper-sonal communication (Bolton, 1979; Gordon, 1980; Johnson & John-son, 1991; Kottkamp, 1990a). Each of these communication forms implicitly and sometimes explicitly communicates the sender's de-sire to change the other, implying that the sender knows what the change should be and how it should come about. Messages like these, although intended to help, merely reinforce the recipient's sense of subordination, helplessness, and incompetence. In some cases, even the use of praise by an instructor can convey a status message: "I, the expert, am using my standards to assess your performance." Because these obstacles to communication are so pervasive in our language, whether in speaking with children, colleagues, or subordinates, it is difficult to develop patterns of speech that encourage the open dialogue and communication that are the essence of reflective prac-tice. It is particularly difficult if we have nagging doubts about the ability of others to assume responsibility for their own learning.

When the facilitator deeply believes that individuals are committed to improving their own performance, willing to assume responsibility for their professional growth, and able to learn, it is more likely that she or he will interact in a positive, constructive, and nonthreatening way with the other participants. If the facilitator trusts the participants, the participants are more likely to return that trust. Trust engenders trust.

(5) People need and want information about their own performance. If we accept the notion that people are willing and able to assume responsibility for their own professional growth, how, then, does that growth come about? One of the key issues in reflective practice revolves around that question.

The literature in the area of adult supervision identifies performance feedback as a critical aspect of the supervisory process. Information about performance—strengths and weaknesses—is essential to continued learning and professional growth. On the other hand, research in different organizational settings, including schools, shows that performance feedback is a neglected aspect of the supervisory process. It is widely accepted that performance feedback is an essential ingredient in professional growth. Nevertheless, in practice, people —business or school administrators, teachers, or students—seldom receive feedback about their performance and even less fre- quently meaningful information that actually leads to professional development (Bridges, 1986; McGregor, 1960; Natriello & Dornbusch, 1984).

Because reflective practice is based on the assumption that changes in behavior are inextricably linked with growing awareness about one's own performance, it is important to examine this discrepancy between our espoused theory and our theory-in-use. What accounts for this breakdown in the supervisory process? Why are professionals so reluctant to share performance information with one another?

Argyris and Schon (1974) provided an explanation for this apparent reluctance to share information openly. From years of research in different organizational settings, they developed a theoretical framework that can be used to interpret behavior in modern organizations.

According to the researchers, two contrasting models or action theories influence interpersonal behavior: Model I and Model II. Model I, they proposed, is a prevailing theory-in-use in modern organizations. One of the main indicators of this action theory is a perceived need to maintain unilateral control. The teacher in the classroom develops instructional management techniques to make sure that the class doesn't get out of hand. The administrator is very careful not to take any actions that upset parents, teachers, or the board of education.

One of the primary ways the individual stays in control is by withholding information. This withholding strategy increases unilateral control in several ways. First, withholding information precludes others from active involvement in decision making. If the administrator withholds information from staff, the knowledge needed to analyze problems, develop strategies, and make decisions remains the exclusive property of the administrator. If the supervisor withholds information about a subordinate's performance, the supervisor retains the right to make decisions about the subordinate's work and progress. Second, withholding information, particularly critical information, prevents conflict. Withholding information presumably reduces the likelihood of confrontation or conflict. Administrators often will not confront a teacher with complaints or a concern about the teacher's performance because of a fear that the teacher will not take it well and create a problem. By withholding information, we keep things calm and under control—*our* control.

Withholding information also responds to a protective need, a sense of social responsibility to others. We withhold critical information because we believe that it hurts other people's feelings and perhaps reduces our own ability to remedy the situation. Obviously, no one likes to hear that their work isn't up to expectations. If we don't believe that people want to be competent and that they want and will use the information to improve their performance, there is little incentive to engage in what is likely to be a difficult conversation.

How we define professional problems affects our attitudes toward the feedback process. When we observe positive actions and effects, we make the assumption that these actions and outcomes are an indicator of professional competence, dedication, or commitment. When we observe less than desirable practice, we often make a judgment—not simply about the act but about the person. Conversations about the senior teacher whose performance has been slipping gradually or even precipitously often lead to a decision to do nothing, or to recommend a transfer, because of the assumption that the problem lies with the person. We believe that the person doesn't care or is incapable of changing at this point in his or her career. With this theory-in-use shaping our actions, it becomes difficult if not impossible to raise certain issues. When we talk about the problem, if we do, we will likely speak in a guarded way, circling around the issue rather than confronting the problem directly. Information is withheld; the problem is kept hidden.

We withhold critical information and avoid discussing problems or concerns because we believe that, in so doing, we will keep things under control, protect ourselves, and keep others from being hurt. In reality, however, this action strategy does not yield the predicted results. In contrast with what we might expect, Model I strategies generate defensive relationships and mistrust. Further, these efforts at unilateral control are disincentives to innovation, organizational commitment, and risk taking. In short, Model I strategies do not support the development of a community committed to professional growth and development; they do not help to build a learning organization (Argyris, 1990; Senge, 1990).

In comparison, Model II encompasses very different beliefs about people and their motivation, suggests very different strategies, and predicts very different outcomes. In Model I, the desire for unilateral control leads to withholding information. In Model II, the belief that control can only be effective when it is achieved through collaborative means is associated with an open flow of information. The Model I action theory anticipates dire consequences as a result of open communication. Model II predicts that openly sharing information will improve the quality of interpersonal relations, stimulate professional growth, and enhance organizational effectiveness.

There is a growing body of research that confirms that Model II is more likely than its counterpart to create the organizational conditions that encourage trust, collaboration, and effective problem solving (Argyris, 1990; Belenky, Clinchy, Goldberger, & Tarule, 1986; Bifano, 1989; Blase & Kirby, 1992; Jentz, 1982; Jentz & Wofford,

1979; Leithwood & Jantzi, 1990; Osterman, 1991; Parkay & Hall, 1992). Nevertheless, there is still a great deal of resistance to open communication, particularly when the message being sent is critical of another person's performance.[1]

Reflective practice requires Model II assumptions and strategies. To engage in reflective practice requires that we rethink those Model I beliefs that counsel us to exercise unilateral control and withhold information. If we assume that problems reflect a lack of motivation or personal weakness, there is no rationale for providing information. On the other hand, if we believe that problems exist because people may not be fully aware of the problem or because they lack information, resources, or support needed to design and implement other strategies, we are more likely to engage in those difficult conversations and name the problems openly.

From this perspective, information about performance, whether positive or negative, is welcome because it gives professionals the knowledge they need to begin to see their own performance clearly and to create change. "When a practitioner becomes a researcher into his [or her] own practice, he [or she] engages in a continuing process of self-education. . . . the recognition of error, with its resulting uncertainty, can become a source of discovery rather than an occasion for self defense" (Schon, 1983, p. 299).

(6) Collaboration enriches professional development. (a) Work in small groups, or cooperative learning, seems to yield higher achievement, more positive relationships, and psychologically healthier members than individualistic learning (Brown et al., 1989a, 1989b; Johnson & Johnson, 1989). These findings seem to be applicable to professional development, in general, and to reflective practice, in particular. Aside from the fact that individuals have access to more information and different perspectives in a group setting, there are other reasons that recommend collaborative approaches to reflective practice. The focus of reflective practice is professional practice. Individuals' practice is influenced by the social environment in the workplace. When other professionals participate in the effort, the work group becomes a culture that supports learning and growth. Describing the importance of teaming for professional development,

Johnson and Johnson (1991, p. 43) concluded that change—in action theories and behavior patterns—is easier and more likely to be permanent when it takes place in a group because the group provides needed emotional support, encouragement, and consensual validation of the changes that occur.

(b) Every semester when we begin group problem-solving activities in administrator preparation courses, students experience discomfort. Many of them have had little experience in working with a group where tasks were actually shared and, of those who have, many remember unpleasant experiences. In these prior situations, typical group patterns prevailed with one or more individuals emerging to assume leadership and to complete the task with minimal input from others. Based on these experiences, their underlying beliefs about the effectiveness of collaboration are weak. For many, these experiences lead them to prefer work settings where individuals directly control the nature and direction of decisions and work.

How the facilitator works with participants will be shaped by the strengths of his or her beliefs about the importance of the group. Of particular importance is the extent to which the facilitator can relinquish individual control and share leadership and learning decisions with the entire group.

KEY STRATEGIES

While beliefs provide the underpinning for the reflective process, far more is required. Through actions and words, the facilitator must convey these beliefs to establish an atmosphere of trust in which people can communicate openly and freely. Increasingly, the professional development literature emphasizes the importance of collegial and collaborative approaches to supervision suggesting that professionals learn most from supervisory approaches where observer and observed work together to develop greater understanding (Gitlin & Bullough, 1989; Gitlin & Smyth, 1989; McLaughlin & Pfeiffer, 1988). In these collegial models, the supervisor, whether superior or peer, engages in a reflective dialogue with a person whose work has been observed. In essence, good supervision and reflective practice are interchangeable; being an effective facilitator requires good supervisory skills. While supervision is often viewed as a dyadic relationship between the supervisor and another individual, reflective practice takes place in a small group setting. Consequently, the facilitator must be able to communicate effectively with individuals in a group setting. There are several specific communication skills and methods that establish trust and facilitate interpersonal communication and collaboration about professional development issues.

The essence of communication is a shared message: One person sends a message and the other person interprets the message as it was intended. There is an exchange of information; there is shared meaning. In simple terms, there is communication when people understand each other. So, while it is important to be able to present one's own point of view (advocacy), it's also important to be able to understand the other person's perspective (inquiry). The effective facilitator combines skills of advocacy and inquiry.[2]

Advocacy

Advocacy involves communication of one's own thoughts, feelings, intentions, and knowledge. Advocacy involves communicating information about oneself and about others. In either case, the communication can and should facilitate reflection.

Self-disclosure. Several recent studies (Blase & Kirby, 1992; Sagor, 1991) found that principals who were able to establish an atmosphere fostering professional development and growth shared a number of characteristics. Foremost among these was "not knowing it all." These principals were people who were willing to admit that they didn't have all the answers and to ask their staffs for help in understanding problems and developing solutions. By admitting to their own fallibility, they were able to generate a sense of openness among their subordinates. The principals made it possible for teachers and staff to discuss problems, and they created atmospheres in which people were able and willing to pool ideas and resources. They created environments in which reflective practice was the norm for professional behavior; they created cultures of reflective practice.

Self-disclosure—the deliberate communication of information about oneself to others—is an important way to establish and maintain trust (Beebe & Masterson, 1990). If the facilitator is willing to engage in reflective analysis of his or her own ideas and to share his or her own imperfect processes, trust is more likely to develop (Belenky et al., 1986).

Descriptive feedback. As Chapter 4 explains in more detail, the facilitator advances the process of reflection by gathering and sharing information about participants' performance. Given the often sensitive nature of the information, the way that the facilitator provides feedback is critical to the success of the process. In general, there are two ways of providing feedback: descriptive and prescriptive. While prescriptive feedback is more likely to be the norm, descriptive feedback is more likely to be effective.

Descriptions are communications that carry messages of fact. They are about what "is" or "was." Prescriptions, in contrast, are communications that carry messages of evaluation. They can be straightforward evaluations in the form of judgments; they can be slightly more oblique as in "you should . . ." or "you ought to . . ." They can also be messages that contain untested assumptions about the motivation of another person, for example, "You were making excuses to the student about . . ." In each case, the sender of the prescription makes a decision for or about the receiver and assumes responsibility and authority to interpret, assess, or direct the other person's behavior. Because they lead to unilateral control and preclude collaboration, prescriptive messages are Model I messages. As such, they block communication and generate defensive behavior. Prescriptive messages are unlikely to be heard and unlikely to encourage reflection. Because prescriptive language predominates in supervisory relationships, developing facility in the use of descriptive feedback is difficult, but not impossible.

The "I-message" is a particularly effective technique for developing descriptive feedback skills. The "I-message" consists of three parts: behavior, feelings, and consequences.

I-message = Behavior + Feelings + Consequences

Behavior/event. This part of the message describes the behavior or event that is troublesome to you. Constructing an I-message is like developing a picture in words so that the other person can see the situation as you see it: literally, framing the problem. The picture of the problem becomes clearer to the extent that the language chosen is as concrete, graphic, and nonevaluative as possible. The message simply describes what is happening as you see it. Its purpose is not to place blame.

Feelings and consequences. The second part of the message describes your feelings about that particular behavior. Is the situation upsetting? As a result, are you angry, concerned, frustrated? The third part of the message explains why the behavior has the effect on you that it does: What are the consequences for you?

To illustrate, consider the parent dealing with the soon-to-be condemned teenager's room. If the parent were to construct an I-message for that situation, it might look like this.

Behavior: Your room is a disaster. There are no clothes left in the closet or the drawers; I haven't been able to find the floor or the furniture in months; the dust is building up to a dangerous level; and the dirty dishes, glasses, and half-filled soda cans are a health hazard.

Feelings: I'm really upset about this

Consequences: because . . .
   (a) you have allergies and are close to an attack;
   (b) I enjoy having a neat and clean home and the sight of your room drives me nearly insane; and
   (c) I'm worried that you aren't developing the habits that you need to be a responsible adult.

The first part of the message conveys a clear description of the problem as you see it, and the second and third parts of the message describe how this behavior or situation affects you personally: How do you feel about it, and what are the consequences for you—as a person, as a parent, or as an administrator? The term *consequences* is sometimes misinterpreted to mean penalties associated with the action: If you don't do this, then this will happen. But, in the I-message, the communication merely describes the situation from your perspective: how you feel about it and what repercussions you fear.

The strictly nonevaluative nature of this format and the personalization of the communication minimizes the other person's defensiveness and sets the stage for open communication and dialogue. While it may not always lead to a successful resolution, it enables people to express their feelings openly without hurting the other person or creating an adversarial, win/lose situation. When this technique is introduced in class, students are asked to try it—in their homes, classrooms, or professional dealings. Because the form of the message reflects Model II assumptions and because our patterns of communication, particularly in conflict situations, too frequently reflect Model I assumptions, students experience difficulty in phrasing the messages unless they have previously received formal training. At the same time, students invariably return with success stories. Typically, the students report a sense of surprise on the part of the other person, who was anticipating criticism and was somewhat startled at the very different nature of this message. In most cases, even difficult situations gave way to dialogue where there had been none before, and often resolution.

Because of its emphasis on descriptive feedback, the I-message facilitates communication: It makes it more likely that the person receiving the information will be able to hear it. The I-message also encourages reflection on the part of the sender as well. On being introduced to the technique, people find they have great difficulty in constructing each stage of the message. They have difficulty in describing the problem so that another person can share their understanding; they also have difficulty in articulating how they feel about the situation and in identifying meaningful consequences. Take, for example, the teacher who is repeatedly late for class. By the time the I-message has been prepared, the administrator is able to state clearly that he or she is concerned about this pattern of behavior because of the impact on the students. Although, in retrospect, this may appear obvious, in the process of constructing the message, it may not be so clear. The format of the I-message requires you to think things through clearly in ways that can be shared. As one administrator described it, the "I-message forces you to look at yourself. When you have to give an I-message, there's a degree of honesty about yourself that you have to have." It encourages you to articulate and examine the assumptions and beliefs you bring to different situations. It requires you to decide how you really feel about things and to determine if what's bothering you really does have important consequences: Are you upset because the teacher's actions affect students or are you upset because the teacher's actions are a challenge to your authority? If the consequences are important and the link between the behavior and the effect is plausible, it is more likely that the listener will be able to "hear" the message and accept the importance of change.

Inquiry

Although the facilitator plays a critical role in conveying information to the participants, an equally important aspect of the role is what Bolman and Deal (1991) describe as inquiry: "behavior whose purpose is to learn what others think, know, want, or feel" (p. 138).

Listening is one of the most important inquiry techniques. Listening, very different than being silent, is a focused activity in which the listener pays close attention to the speaker's message. Texts about interpersonal communication skills describe different modes of listening.[3]

Attentive listening. At the most basic level is attentive listening. Through a combination of posture, gestures, eye contact, nods, and murmurs, the listener "tells" the speaker that she or he is being heard. This sense of being heard has a powerful impact on the course of conversations in the future (Belenky et al., 1986). Listening conveys an impression of interest—and acceptance—and encourages the person to open up even more.

Reflecting is a another method of listening. In the process of reflective listening, the facilitator basically repeats or paraphrases the sender's message to determine how accurately the message was received. On one level, these reflective responses help to clarify the communication and ensure that the sender's message is being received in the way intended. On another level, reflective listening is another way for the facilitator to tell the speaker that her or his message was important enough to warrant close attention. This implicit message provides encouragement for the speaker to continue to probe a little deeper.

The listening or inquiry process is a key to effective facilitation. In this process, the listener (facilitator) must give full attention to the speaker. While the facilitator is actively attending to what the speaker is saying and trying to understand the speaker's point of view and feelings about the issue, there is less opportunity to be thinking about what his or her own response is going to be. As the facilitator develops listening skills, it is more likely that the other members of the group will take a more active role simply because the facilitator is doing the job that's intended—that is, facilitating, being a guide, a reflector.

Questioning. Questioning is another mode of inquiry that encourages reflective practice. After introducing the concepts of reflective practice to a group of business educators, I was approached with a question: "But how do you get people to begin to see their own theories-in-use?" My response at the time was to ask them why. Why did you do it that way? What were you thinking about? Reflective practitioners and those who facilitate the process ask questions. Two researchers who use teachers' stories to encourage reflective practice talk about how they respond "with questions about why the story was told in the way it was. By answering the researcher's question, the participants may penetrate more deeply to other experiences" (Clandinin & Connelly, 1991, p. 268).

A teacher who was involved in a 4-year collaborative project involving university researchers, teachers, and principals described the way this spirit of inquiry looks in practice:

The researchers did not come into our classrooms to recommend changes or to tell us how we might improve. Instead, they approached us with a deep respect for what we knew, a desire to learn what we saw as troublesome in our own teaching, and a methodology that encouraged us to become aware of and to question our own assumptions about our practice. The researchers came into our classrooms to observe, take fieldnotes, share with us what they had found, and ask questions about what they had observed. The questions were non-judgmental, non-critical, accepting, and supportive. We answered the questions, and, in the process, became more aware of our own knowledge. They asked us questions that we knew the answers to; but, until they had asked us the questions, we hadn't thought about the answers. That began to get us to question more things for ourselves. The researchers were not suggesting changes we should make, but by being asked questions and reflecting on them, we discovered ways that we wanted to change. Reflecting on these questions was a real breakthrough for us because we began to question our own assumptions. Why had we not asked ourselves those questions before? We had been overwhelmed by the complex task of teaching in the traditional style that did not include opportunities to observe or experience reflection. (Berkey et al., 1990, p. 213)

Sagor's (1991) study concluded that, by asking "probing questions which go to the heart of the teaching/learning process" (p. 15) and by gathering information about professional practice, principals established a norm of inquiry and experimentation. By acting as facilitators rather than experts, by providing information and support, they allowed teachers in these schools to feel empowered and to act with efficacy in developing new and more effective instructional policies and practices on an individual and schoolwide basis.

In the organizational setting, the facilitator is the technical assistant, the person who tilts the mirror so that it reflects from a different angle, the person who focuses the microscope so that an undistinguishable entity comes into view, the person who turns the prism or kaleidoscope or changes the lens from telescopic to wide angle so that the observer sees the same phenomenon from many different perspectives. Questions are one of the tools that the facilitator uses to shift the perspective.

Not all types of questions are appropriate, however. Questions that are likely to foster reflective practice are those that reflect an openness to ideas and information and a desire to develop a deeper understanding of events and meanings from the other person's perspective. Questions that have the opposite effect will be those questions that try to place the blame, questions that have an answer waiting in the wings, or questions that interrupt and distract rather than complement and enrich. Questions encourage reflective practice in another way as well. They encourage individuals to think more deeply about their own experience, and they also serve to focus attention on those issues that are most important to the practitioner. Sagor (1991) described this as another means of buffering: insulating practitioners from the everyday, but often trivial, distractions of the workplace.

Group Process Skills

It is important to remember that reflective practice often takes place in a group context. While the skills described above are important for facilitating interpersonal communication whether in a one-to-one or a small group situation, there are additional skills the facilitator needs to work effectively with a small group. One of the reasons for describing reflective practice as a collaborative activity is the belief that professionals can learn more if they share their learning experience with others. The facilitator's role in the process is not to provide content expertise but to create an environment that supports cooperative learning. To the extent that other professionals contribute their knowledge and experience, the process will be richer. Consequently, the facilitator must be skilled at developing an environment in which the participants feel comfortable enough to contribute actively (safety) and an environment in which they have the opportunity to participate (equity). Furthermore, the facilitator must attend to the task and socioemotional needs of the group members, ensuring that the group experiences a sense of accomplishment and that the personal feelings of the group members are heeded.[4]

SUMMARY

In sum, then, one of the most important elements in the reflective practice environment is trust. Without authorization and support from organizational superiors (the buffer), it is unlikely that reflective practice will take place, let alone flourish. Once this organizational permission is secured, the role of the facilitator is vitally important in creating an environment conducive to reflection. In keeping with the experiential model of learning that was outlined in Chapter 2, the successful facilitator will be distinguished by an ability to engage individuals in a challenging learning process. Emphasizing professional development beliefs and communication skills, an advertisement for a facilitator might look like this:

Position Available: Facilitator for Reflective Practice
A person who's inherently curious, someone who doesn't have all the answers and isn't afraid to admit it, someone who is confident enough in his or her ability to be able to accept challenges in a nondefensive manner; someone who is secure enough to make his or her own thinking public and therefore subject to discussion; someone who's a good listener; someone who likes and trusts other people to make the right decisions if given the opportunity; someone who is able to see things from another's perspective and is sensitive to the needs and feelings of others; someone who is able to relax and lean back and let others assume the responsibility for their own learning. Some experience desirable but not as important as the ability to learn from mistakes.

NOTES

1. Jentz's books (Jentz, 1982; Jentz & Wofford, 1979) include several case studies that illustrate the difficulty that administrators experience when trying to adopt Model II assumptions in their supervisory conversations with staff members. These case studies

also illustrate the dramatic positive effects that the Model II strategies elicit.

2. Bolman and Deal (1991) have developed a model illustrating how these two communication techniques are central to Model II and facilitate interpersonal communication and problem solving.

3. *People Skills* by Robert Bolton (1979) provides a thorough treatment of those communication skills that are so integral to reflective practice.

4. Doyle and Straus (1982) provide a detailed and easy-to-understand explanation of the role of the facilitator and its impact on group process.

4

Developing a Reflective Perspective: Gathering Information

The term *reflective practice* is interpreted and understood in different ways. As we view it, reflective practice is a means of change, a process through which practitioners can discover what they already understand and know how to do (self-awareness) and a way of discovering new and better ways of doing things (change). In short, reflective practice is a professional development strategy designed to enable professionals to change their behavior, thereby improving the quality of their performance.

Within the reflective practice model, awareness is essential for behavioral change. To gain a new level of insight into personal behavior, the reflective practitioner assumes a dual stance being, on one hand, the actor in a drama and, on the other hand, the critic who sits in the audience watching and analyzing the entire performance. From this perspective, the individual comes to a new understanding of his or her own behavior. She or he develops a conscious awareness of personal goals and stated intentions (espoused theories), and, through observation and analysis of actions, comes to identify the ideas, or theories-in-use, that guide the strategic choices. As understanding grows in each of these areas, the practitioner becomes more adept at assessing performance relative both to intentions and to outcomes.

This chapter describes some of the means that can be used to stimulate the reflective perspective and, specifically, to gather information about espoused theories and theories-in-use.

GATHERING INFORMATION ABOUT ESPOUSED THEORIES

Exploring this aspect of behavior is relatively easy because espoused theories are reflected in what people say. To examine espoused theories—about education, about administration, about supervision—we ask people to write or talk about these issues. There are a variety of ways to gather this information; below are accounts of ways that have proven effective in working with practicing educators.

Educational and Administrative Platforms

A platform is a written statement that expresses one's stated beliefs, values, orientations, goals, and, occasionally, the assumptions that guide professional practice. More colloquially, it is one's philosophy of education or administration, a concise statement of what one intends to do, to accomplish, and how (Kottkamp, 1982, 1990a; Sergiovanni & Starratt, 1983).

While all platform statements fit this basic description, the form of the platform may differ depending on the particular context. Kottkamp, for example, uses platform development as part of his course "The Reflective Administrator." The students are teachers, administrators, and prospective administrators with different interests and levels of experience. As their initial assignment, students develop a two-part platform based on Sergiovanni and Starratt's work (1983). The first part, the Educational Platform, is about teaching, learning, and its context. The Administrative/Supervisory Platform is about the orientations and means used to support and facilitate the educational part. Students are encouraged to write contextualized platforms grounded in their experiences and to consider this as a realistic rather than a hypothetical exercise.

The assignment asks that students ground their platforms in real experience, but the details of form and content are purposely kept open. (See Chapter 5 for more detail.) The students have the widest latitude in deciding how to approach the development of their own platforms. For those who require some direction or structure, topics suggested by Sergiovanni and Starratt (1983) are offered: aims of education, image of the learner, value of the curriculum, image of the teacher, preferred student-teacher relationship, purpose of supervision, and preferred process of supervision.

Following the guidelines of Sergiovanni and Starratt, Kottkamp prefers a relatively open-ended approach to the platform that allows the practitioner a great deal of flexibility in determining the structure and the context; others use a more structured approach. Barnett and Brill (1989), for example, use the platform as a key component of an intensive principal preparation program. During the course of the program, the aspiring principals develop a platform addressing the components in the Framework for Instructional Leadership developed by Bossert, Dwyer, Rowan, and Lee (1982): student outcomes, instructional climate, instructional organization, principal's routine behaviors, community, personal beliefs and experiences, institutional context, current preparation, and future preparation and development. In preparing the platform, for example, the educator describes the types of skills, attitudes, and feelings he or she wants students to possess; the type of climate needed to support these outcomes; how instruction will be organized and delivered to support the desired climate and student outcomes; the activities that the principal will adopt to ensure that types of instructional organization, climate, and student outcomes will actually occur; how parents will be involved in school affairs; and the type of support they will request from district personnel or other sources.

The prospective administrators also describe their philosophy of education and consider how they will communicate it to various members of the school community. The platform statement concludes with reflection on the experiences that have most influenced their development as future administrators and the types of experiences they would like to obtain in the future.

Osterman uses a similar structured model when working with students. Describing the platform as a "mission statement," she asks them to outline their vision or describe their ideal school in terms of learning, instruction, governance, school climate, and school community relations. In this statement, they describe their goals for students; how they envision the learning process; the type of school climate conducive to effective teaching and learning; the way the school will be governed and thereby the nature of the relationships between and among teachers, administrators, students, parents, central office, and other members of the community. With their vision articulated, the principals proceed to the next step: to identify the action strategies that they as administrators will adopt to enable this vision to become reality.

An even more focused form of the platform is the miniplatform, which is typically used within the context of a particular exercise or activity. For example, after giving the actors the background information in a role-play situation, the facilitator asks them to write a brief statement of their goals for the activity (what they hope to accomplish) as well as a brief description of their plan of action (what they intend to do).[1]

Issues related to platform format. There are several considerations in deciding among the various platform formats. The facilitator has a great deal of flexibility in how the platform task is introduced. The choice of how to proceed can be influenced by a number of factors including the purpose of the activity, the length of time available, and the composition of the group. In Kottkamp's reflective administrator course, the purpose is to introduce the general notion of reflective practice and to provide the students with an experiential understanding of the concept and the basic skills needed to engage in reflective practice. The students who enroll in this course are all educators but bring to the course far different perspectives and experiences: personal, educational, and professional. A relatively unstructured introduction to the platform seems appropriate given the divergent interests and needs of the group.

In other situations, a more structured approach may be preferred. At Hofstra, students in the administrative preparation program prepare platforms at several points in the program addressing different issues. For example, in a course dealing with schools as social organizations, the platform focuses on the student's vision of the school environment as a workplace for teachers and students. In professional development, too, the objectives of the participants may warrant a structured focus. In the principal renewal project described in Chapter 6, the principals crafted platforms dealing with core issues of their practice.

Whatever model the facilitator chooses carries with it an implicit statement of values and beliefs. As the platform becomes more structured, it is more likely to influence the way the individual responds. For example, in a relatively open-ended approach, prospective administrators might discover that they had neglected to discuss school governance, making the assumption that it was the sole province of the building principal. When governance is identified as a category that must be addressed, the facilitator and the respondent lose this opportunity to discover and uncover certain surprises. On the other hand, this opportunity is gained at a cost of considerably increased ambiguity about the task. Where time is short, more direction may be warranted.

While writing a platform or mission statement has reflective value beyond simply attaining a statement of espoused theory, there are other ways of eliciting the information needed to construct the basic elements of an individual's espoused theory. With these other methods, a facilitator or event is used to bring forth the needed information.

Interviews

One straightforward method of capturing espoused theory is to interview an individual for that purpose, posing questions such as the following:

As (name of role), what are some of your most important goals and priorities?

Of the things that you do, which do you consider to be the most important?

What are beliefs and values about the aspects of your work that you have named as most important to you?

How do you go about attempting to accomplish your goals? What are your methods of working toward these goals?

How would you describe your philosophy as an educator?

What are the biggest problems you face in your work?

How do you believe these should be resolved?

These questions are only suggestions. The important thing is to engage the interviewee in an honest and deep conversation about his or her goals, ideals, beliefs, values, intentions, and desired orientations toward the work. With a little practice, espoused theory can be elicited from most individuals in a fairly short time. The questions and conversation need to be adapted to the individual; the facilitator and the practitioner can work together to frame questions and seek answers.

Documents and Statements

Sometimes espoused theories can be found in statements or documents an individual has prepared for another purpose. Examples of such sources include the first speech prepared for the faculty by a new principal, a short statement made to the PTA, statements made to the board of education by a superintendent, a collection of short pieces written over a period of time for a newsletter, regular communication to parents, or journal entries. Such information may prove sufficient to elicit an espoused theory or may be the beginning point for gathering more information through an interview or for asking the individual to develop a platform. Later, we will describe how similar documents can be used to identify theories-in-use. To the extent that documents are prepared in a self-conscious way, it is more likely that the espoused theory will be presented, as in the situation where a new principal faces the faculty members knowing full well that she is expected to convey her philosophy and that her words will be carefully scrutinized.

Case Studies

Activities that require a cognitive response tend to tap espoused beliefs. When individuals analyze a case study, for example, they use their cognitive and analytic capabilities; they discuss what others should have done or what they themselves might have done. These analytic responses are not necessarily accurate predictors of behavior in a real situation; if confronted with a similar situation, they might act in a very different way than what they *think* they would or than they would like. In these typically prescriptive or evaluative responses, we see "thinking" but not action. Nevertheless, these activities are an important way to capture espoused theory because the responses reflect our conscious values and beliefs. These spontaneous responses translate readily into more general statements of belief, intent, and value.

Espoused Theory: Summing Up

In this section, we have concentrated on ways to gather information about espoused theories. Having articulated a statement of philosophy including beliefs, values, and goals, individuals can then begin a conscious process of reflection in which they begin to assess the nature and effects of their own observable behavior. In many cases, discrepancies between actions and stated intentions will become readily apparent. These inconsistencies—these surprises— rivet the learners' attention and engage them wholeheartedly in the learning process. We have highlighted the platform as a means of eliciting the espoused theory because it is a method that involves the individual to the fullest and because it typically initiates other aspects of reflection.

Although information about espoused theories can be gathered through dialogue and conversation as well as through writing, because the act of writing one's thoughts seems to have a substantially different and greater impact, we recommend that these oral statements be used as the stimulus for writing. Being required to "name" the reality in written form seems to interject another level of reflection beyond that required to express one's thoughts orally. Aside from the value of writing to heighten personal insight and understanding, the written platform can serve as a bench mark against which one can measure and assess change; the written platform also serves, as one administrator described it, as something to hang your hat on— a reminder of where you stand when the going gets rough.

GATHERING INFORMATION ABOUT THEORIES-IN-USE

The second step in facilitating the reflective process focuses on theories-in-use. Ultimately, it is these personal action theories that we want to understand. Because these beliefs are so deeply ingrained in our consciousness, with few exceptions, individuals can rarely articulate them. They know the theories at a tacit level but may not be able to express them in words. As part of the Reflective Practice Seminar (see Chapter 6), Osterman arranged an interview with an unusually successful principal in the New York City School system to find out what he had done to turn a depressed and low-achieving school into a truly "effective" school. The interview yielded little information as the principal, a highly intelligent and verbal individual, had difficulty describing his own role in the transformation. Because of this phenomenon, eliciting theories-in-use requires a different tack. Because it is so difficult for people to articulate the reasons behind their actions, we must construct a portrait of these theories by observing behavior. By gathering information about behavior, we stop the action so that the practitioner and others can stand back and look more carefully at what was done. By examining what was done, it is then possible to detect the assumptions that prompted the behavior.

While this process of extrapolating theories-in-use from observable behavior sounds quite complex, in reality, we are all relatively skilled in this type of analysis. Parkay and Hall (1992), for example, provide us with a profile of a new principal where this incongruence between espoused theory and theory-in-use was clearly evident.

Herb was a new principal who came into his position "espousing values based on collaboration, empowerment, and trust" (p. 216). Initially excited and enthusiastic about the opportunity to participate in school leadership in a meaningful way, the teachers soon realized that, even though Herb talked a good line, in reality, he was far more comfortable with a highly autocratic style of leadership. Without prior notice or discussion, he issued directives establishing rigid behavioral guidelines for teachers and relied on coercive disciplinary measures with his staff, often overreacting in situations that seemed to threaten his authority. Despite what he said, it was quite clear that Herb was unable to interact with his staff in the collaborative manner that he espoused. In sharp contrast to the environment of trust that he hoped to create, he created instead a climate characterized by tension, mistrust, and anger.

Although Herb genuinely wished to create a collaborative environment, he was unable to do so. At the root of his behavior were theories-in-use that prompted him to act in ways that were totally ineffective in achieving his stated intentions. If Herb were able to stand back and see his behavior as the teachers and others saw it, it is possible that he would see the inconsistencies between his words and actions. With this new insight, it would be possible for him to explore the assumptions that led him to act in such an autocratic and coercive manner, to contrast those with his espoused views, and eventually to consider other modes of behavior. The critical step in this change scenario then is observational information. Without access to this feedback, it is unlikely that Herb would comprehend the nature and impact of his practice and, if asked, would continue to aver his collaborative approach to leadership.

To facilitate reflective practice then, we need not only to describe espoused theories but to develop a clear understanding of the theories-in-use that shape individual behavior. To detect and examine these elusive theories-in-use requires observation; we must position the mirror in such a way that the professional can step outside the action to watch. The following section outlines several methods of collecting behavioral descriptions to help individuals develop this reflective perspective.

Direct Observation

The most direct means to gather information about behavior is through observation. To determine how people act and the assumptions that prompt their actions, you watch them. Another person—superior or peer—comes into the work setting and simply watches the person at work, a practice that is a regular component of most teacher evaluation systems.

Shadowing. Although administrators' performance is not directly observed as part of the evaluation process, the technique of shadowing offers a parallel. In the Peer-Assisted Leadership (PAL) program, for example, pairs of principals observe one another during the course of their work and conduct reflective interviews with each other (Barnett, 1990). Whatever the setting, another person observes the action, keeps notes, and subsequently meets with the person being observed to provide descriptive, nonevaluative feedback.

Videotaping. Video technology is a highly effective means of gathering information about the nature of practice. After a period of time to allow the person to become accustomed to this strange set of eyes, the video camera records the individual at work. This technique is unusually effective because it provides an unfiltered and true record of events without any possibility of bias from the observer. Kathryn Zietlow, a first-grade teacher in the Teacher Development and Organizational Change Project (TDOC), offered an interesting illustration of the impact of this technology:

The researcher I worked most closely with, Doug Campbell, had communicated to me, in journal entries, about the productive things that were going on in my classroom, but I was not seeing the same things he was seeing until I watched a video of my class.

I had begun having my students create their own sentences and stories by using a certain list of words that we formulated together and listed on the chalkboard. One day a week, at reading group time, they came back with their stories to share with other children in the group. I was sitting at the table with them, and I thought I was watching what was happening. What I saw, as I sat there, was fidgeting, what I heard was noise. It did not seem as if anyone was paying attention to anyone reading. Until I watched the video. To my amazement, I saw first graders leaning over the table, pointing to the words on the paper, and asking the reader/writer about the story. I saw interaction among the group members, many interested faces, and a very productive activity. It was quite an insight to realize that what I had valued —or thought that I had valued—as a necessary learning environment was hindering some very important student involvement. I discovered that student activity level and noise were appropriate, productive, and necessary for learning. (Berkey et al., 1990, p. 218)

One outgrowth of this experience, she explained, was a change in the curriculum, with much greater use of student learning centers.

Audiotapes. While limited to the audio portion of behavior, tape recordings also can be very effective in gathering information about individual behavior. In the administrative preparation program at Hofstra, faculty place a great deal of emphasis on developing effective group process skills. In the process of completing a major group task, one group decided to tape one of its sessions. The playback of that tape proved particularly enlightening for one group member who hadn't realized the extent to which she dominated the conversation in the group. For her, the opportunity to hear how she sounded to others was an eye-opener and an incentive to change.

Role Plays

We can also observe behavior in artificial situations by constructing or arranging role plays. In a role play or simulation, the participants are given information about a problem or an event and asked to respond. The ensuing action can range from developing an action agenda (as in a planning meeting) to taking action (handling a supervisory matter or deciding on staff or budget cuts).

Role plays can be done in different ways to achieve different levels of involvement. The facilitator can structure a hypothetical situation designed to examine certain issues. For example, if a practitioner were concerned about the effectiveness of his or her ability to relate to parents, the facilitator might present a related problem and ask the participants to decide how they would respond and enact an encounter. A second way is to derive the role-play situations from the experience of the practitioner. In other words, ask the practitioner to think about a troubling encounter with a parent and then to describe the situation. In explaining the nature of the problem and the events that occurred, the practitioner focuses specifically on his or her own actions and reactions. Given this information, the practitioner then reenacts the situation with one or more other persons who, along with the facilitator or other observers, provide feedback to the practitioner about his or her behavior and its impact on them (see Chapter 5).

Another interesting way of uncovering theories-in-use is to ask individuals to approach the same task from different role perspectives and then to compare the actions and assumptions that seem to accompany the different roles. It is remarkable and eye opening to see how easily individuals shift their behavior to fit a preconceived notion of what is required by a particular role.

Brookfield (1992) described another activity, scenario analysis, in which learners analyze the assumptions that they think underlie the behavior of characters in hypothetical situations. In this exercise, participants are introduced to the process of identifying assumptions but need not focus on their own behavior.

Although artificial in the sense that the action is taking place in the equivalent of a small group laboratory, role plays tend to be surprisingly effective. In the space of a few minutes, the actors become deeply involved in the situation and their characters. The emerging action is far more than a cognitive response; it reflects deeply held beliefs as well as emotions. In the midst of action, habits dominate and the theory-in-use comes into play.

The contrived role play is valuable, but, in our experience, the re-enactment of an actual situation is more powerful. In the former, the behavior serves to identify theories-in-use and provides the basis for reflection and learning, but, because of the contrived nature, it is possible for the practitioner to dismiss the experience as an aberration. Reenactments carry more weight because the person is able to assess the validity of the experience by comparing it with the actual situation. Even in these situations, it is possible for the individual to deny the information that is presented.

Narratives

Narratives can be another form of reenactment if they are descriptive reports of action. Reconstruction of events is far different than an analysis and draws on a different set of skills. A narrative simply tells what happened. Schon (1983) and others talk about how difficult it is for practitioners to articulate craft knowledge. Reconstructing a particular situation is an equally difficult task, requiring the respondent to step back, to chronicle the events, and to describe the actions and reactions of all of the participants including the self.

The facts of the narrative may not be supported by other participants; but the purpose here is not to establish the facts, it is to learn about the individual practitioner. The story presents the perspective of the narrator; it represents his or her experience. In examining the story, we see the events as the narrator saw them; we see what was seen and perhaps what was omitted; we see what was important and what was insignificant.

These narratives can be developed orally or in writing; they can be structured or unstructured. Mattingly (1991), for example, described the use of unstructured oral storytelling in which professionals told stories about their work and analyzed them, investigating underlying values and assumptions.

Journals. The journal is another form of narrative writing that is used extensively to gather information about professional practice and personal action theories.[2] The daily journal, used extensively in teacher and administrator preparation programs, is a running account of important events and interactions that take place in the work setting. Individuals use the journal to describe and raise questions about their experiences and often share their thoughts on a formal or informal basis with other members of their learning group and the instructor or facilitator.

In some cases, the journal assignment may be more focused and structured. Barnett and Brill (1989), for example, use both a daily and a critical incident journal. For the latter, they provide students with a common format: (a) a brief summary description of a meaningful incident, (b) important questions generated by the event, (c) a list of new jargon or concepts, (d) subjective reactions to the incident, (e) a description of what they learned and how it might alter their future responses (p. 10).

In another form, Kelsey (in press) incorporates journal writing in his course, "Problem Analysis and Formulation Skills for Administrators," requiring that students reflect on at least one class event each day. He outlines his expectations to stimulate the quality of their entries:

> What is necessary is that the entries should show that you have done some thinking about each day's work (why it did or did not turn a light on for you, its relation to something else you have read, or experienced, or learned in another class, or . . . etc., etc.) and that the thoughts provoked are not entirely banal!

Whatever form is adopted, the journal is an effective means to obtain information about professional practice and personal action theories.

Case records. Osterman (1991) described the use of a structured and written format called the "case record." A technique developed by Silver (1986) and modified by Osterman (1991), the case record is a format for creating a structured narrative about a problem situation. In addressing a series of questions, the respondent describes the problem and the actions taken to resolve the problem. Several other questions prompt a reflective analysis of the thoughts and intentions that prompted the action and its impact: What were your objectives? What did you hope to accomplish? Were your actions effective? Why or why not?[3]

CASE RECORD FORMAT

1. The Problem
Who was involved? What was the pertinent background information? What was your role in the problem?

2. Outcome/Objectives Desired
What did you hope to accomplish?

3. Alternatives Considered
What alternatives did you consider to solve the problem?

4. Strategies Implemented
What action did you take in an attempt to achieve your objectives?

5. Results
Were your objectives achieved? What happened as a result of your actions?

6. Assessment
Did your plan work as intended? What critical events, decisions, situations influenced the outcome? What would you do differently, if anything?

Autobiography. Autobiographical experience offers another means of gathering information about personal assumptions and theories. Using this approach, Brookfield (1992) outlined an activity he calls "Heroes and Villains." In this exercise, participants identify people whom they regard as exemplary or the reverse and describe aspects of their practice that they admire or find distressing. In three-person groups, one tells the story and the detectives try to uncover the assumptions underlying the storyteller's descriptions. After they generate a list of the assumptions, they test their ideas, trying to generate alternative explanations. Brookfield recommends this strategy as a low risk means of introducing reflective practice: It engages people in thinking about theories-in-use but is not as threatening as a direct focus on personal practice.

Content Analysis

Behavior may be "observed" using written materials produced in the course of normal professional activity. We may examine memos, formal correspondence, lesson plans, meeting schedules, supervision and evaluation reports, newsletters, notices sent to parents, minutes or notes taken at meetings, and other artifacts. These documents would be examined when they provide data directly relevant to assessing their congruence with espoused theory. For example, a principal might espouse teacher involvement in decision making. A check of meeting schedules and minutes, a personal appointment calendar, or memos might be useful. A schedule that did not include time for departmental or faculty meetings, for instance, would be telling.

In an actual case, an administrator wrote a platform espousing a humane, open, and democratic orientation toward subordinates. When he made a careful study of memos that he had sent out over a period of time, however, he was startled to find that the autocratic tone of many of the documents was quite the opposite of what he intended to convey. Having uncovered the discrepancy, he had a focus for changing behavior as well as a means for continuing to monitor it.

Personal Inventories

Another often useful look at behavior may be gotten through personal inventories and diagnostic, counseling, or even research instruments. These provide information on particular attitudes, perceptual or assumptional frames, and other aspects of behavior. While such inventories do not always provide concrete behavioral reports focused directly on some area of inquiry and reflection, they often lead to provocative surprises and help direct attention to a search for specific behaviors. For example, feedback from a research instrument on tolerance and intolerance of ambiguity (Budner, 1962) may be useful in sparking reflective inquiry into supervisory and other behaviors in the ambiguous context of administration.

Students in administrative preparation courses have found feedback from the Myers-Briggs Type Indicator (Myers & McCaulley, 1985) useful and meaningful both in understanding their espoused theories and in highlighting behavioral areas for observation. Based on Jungian psychological concepts, this instrument provides information on how the individual tends to process information, focus attention, and come to decisions. It focuses on the individual's strengths and has been widely used in counseling among high school, college, theological, business, and nursing students and for organizational development work in schools, universities, corporations, and social service agencies.

Barnett and Brill (1989) use Kolb's (1985) Learning Style Inventory to give their principal preparation students information about the particular stages of experiential learning they are most likely to employ.

Christine Johnston (1992) has pioneered the use of the Kolbe Conative Index (KCI) (Kolbe, 1990) in reflective work with administrative teams. *Conation,* which has received relatively little attention in education, is a domain of mind separate from the cognitive and affective domains. Conation has to do with volition, will, what we naturally do and avoid doing, how we respond and perform. The KCI measures intensity within four modes of conation: fact finder, follow through, quick start, and implementor. By combining intensity levels of the four dimensions, the developer has been able to predict behavior, success, and stress in various job categories and work groups. This instrument has considerable value in providing information about behaviors in committees and other task settings.

While many of these examples are most useful for gathering information about individual orientations, attitudes, and assumptions, sharing of information from them can be very helpful in group work, whether the groups are artificially constructed in a course or actual organizational work groups. There are also useful instruments for gathering data on group behavior that can be found within the tradition of organizational development and survey feedback. Old and excellent sources for such instruments include Schmuck and Runkel's (1972) *Handbook of Organizational Development in Schools.*

SUMMARY

In sum, the reflective process begins with experience. By examining what is said and done, it is possible to identify espoused theories and the more elusive theories-in-use. While espoused theories can be identified rather easily through dialogue and writing, the identification of theories-in-use requires action. Toward this end, there are a variety of means that can be used to bring action and experience into the classroom, each of which can be adapted in an almost limitless number of ways to meet the special needs and interests of the participants. By carefully observing behavior, theories-in-use become more apparent and the stage is set for reflection.

NOTES

1. Jentz (1982) outlined a very powerful role-play activity that uses this strategy to reveal Model I assumptions.
2. There is an extensive literature on the use of journals to stimulate reflection at all levels of education including professional preparation. Clift, Houston, and Pugach (1990) offer interesting descriptions of the use of journals as well as other reflective methods for teacher preparation.
3. The first four questions in the case record format also can be used to facilitate planning. Rather than describing events that already have taken place, the respondent thinks about what she or he wants to do. If used in this way, the case record is a platform statement and reflects espoused theories.

5 The Process in Practice: Preparing Reflective Administrators

For over a dozen years, I have offered courses in learning to reflect as part of administrative preparation programs at two universities.[1] When this work began, I could argue that a wholly social science-based program lacked important elements of self-knowledge needed for effective administrative performance (Kottkamp, 1982). Today, the argument for reflection is more complete, essentially the first two chapters of this book. Thus the evolution of courses in reflective practice is an object lesson in the very principles about which we are writing. At the beginning, I could espouse only at an incomplete level. I was guided by what I could say, by my tacit theory-in-use, and by a good deal of faith and risk taking in developing and transforming the courses. Now, having studied my own practice and reflected on my work, I am able to explain in a more complete way the theory-in-use and the what, how, and why guiding my behavior.

When students ask me what the course is about, I say that it is likely my greatest contribution to the field, that I am very enthusiastic about it because what the students learn is likely to have more impact on their professional practice than anything else in their program, that the focus is solidly self-learning rather than learning about things "out there," that they will be looking carefully at their own philosophies and professional practices, and that the major vehicle for doing this is the writing and testing of a platform. I explain that they achieve these ends through writing, thinking, role plays, simulations, and especially through discussing and sharing closely and collaboratively with a small group of peers. I explain that the major reason for doing this is to improve their practice through putting them more in touch with, and therefore gaining control over, their own behaviors in the work setting.

THE PLATFORM

The central element in the course is writing and testing a platform or writing one's espoused theory and then comparing it with observable behavior. Working on these two issues in small groups of four or five takes more than two thirds of the class time. Participants are teachers and administrators enrolled in certification and doctoral programs. They come from diverse roles and experiences and are headed for different futures. Of the various kinds of platforms described in Chapter 4, I opt for a relatively open-ended format. I suggest possible issues as a provisional structure—such as aims of education, major student achievements, social significance of learning, image of the learner, value of the curriculum, image of the teacher, preferred pedagogy, preferred student-teacher relationship, preferred school climate, goal of administration/supervision, preferred process of administration/supervision (see Sergiovanni & Starratt, 1983)— but encourage writing authentically self-representative statements rather than ones constructed around a particular format, model, or authority. I also provide them with my own platform for the course (see Figure 5.1).

Figure 5.1. Robert Kottkamp's Platform for the Reflective Administrator Course

---

Assumptions About Administrative Work

The worlds in which administrators/supervisors work are characterized by ambiguity and immediacy and are heavily value laden. There are few or no ultimate touchstones of success.

The world of each administrator is unique. This is so in part because the setting, environment, constituents, clients, and role partners are unique. It is so in part because each individual constructs his or her own world or reality. (No two of us in the same setting "see" exactly the same dynamics, forces, and things; no two of us are likely to take exactly the same courses of action.)

There is a body of social science knowledge, the models and theories of which are abstractions and which partially "fit" many situations but never fully explicate any particular professional situation. Further, this knowledge base does not tell us how to act in a particular situation. It is useful in "seeing" what is occurring in situations, in "seeing" possibilities, potentials, and estimating some likely outcomes of actions. But, in the end, a professional is "condemned" to take action in a state of ambiguity and uncertainty.

There is probably no "one best way" of doing most things, especially complex things in complex situations.

There is in most professional positions enough "wiggle room" for the individual to define a "vision" of what he or she wishes to do within the organization and where she or he wants to take it. To exercise initiative and to create a vision is to move toward a prophesy that has some chance of self-fulfillment; it is to be an active participant in reconstructing the behavioral world in his or her own image. Given the real constraints in any situation, there are still possibilities. Many administrators do not view their worlds this way; many wait for others to tell them what their role is and never go to the point of owning it and initiating themselves.

Assumptions About Learning

Individuals are more likely to change their behaviors when they perceive incongruities between what they intend, espouse, and base their identities on and their actual behaviors or resulting consequences. Information descriptively delivered is more likely to facilitate behavioral change than information prescriptively delivered.

Learning situations in which the learner perceives the addressing of personal needs and in which she or he may actively engage are likely to result in changes in the learner.

The Course

The intent of the course is to provide a "safe" setting in which students may inquire into the congruency between their intentions and their actual behaviors. My belief is that students will use this opportunity to inquire into themselves.

I value reflective administrators over nonreflective ones because I believe individuals who reflect on their own actions, intentions, and results are both more active in their roles and more likely to be self-corrective in their practice.

My major roles in the course are to structure situations that provide opportunities for students to inquire into themselves, to give valid, descriptive feedback, and to support individuals emotionally; my minor role is to present information.

I intend to create a climate or behavioral world that conforms more to the assumptions of Argyris and Schon's Model II than their Model I (which I believe is normative for many of our work and other worlds and prevents us from seeing ourselves in ways that might be useful for making decisions about our behaviors).

Dilemmas

For me there is always a tension between trusting students with their own intellectual and emotional struggles, and therefore not intervening, and a proclivity to play "savior" by assuming the "teaching/telling" or information giving role.

Personal Note

Writing this was not comfortable. I feel that it is fragmented and incomplete. I feel the press of time. I feel a level of frustration. I also feel good that I have done what I was able to do and that I am willing to show it to you. I trust that I too will receive feedback through the course

Writing the platform. Students write a preliminary platform and then revise it after reading and responding to other platforms (in a very particular way described below) and after my response to them. They are less or more comfortable with the open format depending upon their level of tolerance of ambiguity and other traits.

Although the platform is only espoused theory, writing it usually begins a reflective process of greater depth. Writing itself has the potential to be a powerfully reflective process (Emig, 1977; Kottkamp, 1990a). When writing, we often pause, cycle back, reread, and rethink the very descriptions and ideas we are formulating, and we capture our thought processes in a product to which we may return to reassess, search for options, and plan for the future. I favor an open-ended platform because students tell me they spend a great deal of time formulating their statements. Without a template, they must think long and hard about what is of greater and lesser importance, what is central and what peripheral. They force themselves to do considerable thinking about what they believe, value, and hope to accomplish. Inevitably, they make comparisons with actions taken; they plant the seeds for continued and direct searches for congruity and incongruity between intention and action while creating the platform.

The platform writing *process* as well as the statements themselves are shared in small groups. After I explain the idea of the platform, groups receive many different sample anonymous platforms written by students in prior years as a guide to the basic idea. I encourage them to discuss the process of writing itself and any concerns they have before beginning. I have them trade phone numbers and encourage calls back and forth or to me if they feel really stuck. I report what prior writers have said time and again: Struggling with and writing a platform is one of the most difficult tasks they have ever undertaken. It is an emotional process bringing on alternating feelings of the heights and the "pits." I give them "permission" to feel this way and assure them that they are "normal" and that their feelings are shared by at least one other—if not half the group. I wish them well and reiterate Shakespeare's admonition: "To thine own self be true." Excerpts from platforms in Figure 5.2 indicate how platforms differ depending on person and context.

As they have been told it will be, students find platform writing a valuable experience, but also, as one current student commented: "Writing the platform was *very* difficult. It was a very emotional experience." In working with more than 300 persons on platforms, I found that very few have ever set down their educational beliefs, values,

Figure 5.2. Excerpts From Platforms Showing Diversity in Format and Content

---

The Old Testament states that those who educate others unto justice shall shine as stars for all eternity.

Education unto justice for all: the rich, the poor, the sound and the disabled, the young and the old, regardless of race, creed, or dominant language.

Equal education is not necessarily just or fair education. Justice requires education according to need. As a physician treats each patient according to need, the true teacher educates each student according to needs defined by aptitude, achievement levels, family support, motivation, and individual interests.

Education unto justice requires that spark of creativity that sets up a current of understanding between the student and the world in which she or he lives. It requires a kind of bifocal approach that establishes appreciation for the cultural heritage of the past and also develops the inner strength and flexibility to face the future making the changes necessary to live in the twenty-first century. . . .

Education unto justice requires parent and community involvement contributing the relevance and enrichment needed to provide education that uses not only the traditional educational materials but also the resources of the community at large so that education is not limited to the four walls of the classroom but extends as far as our vision permits. . .

* * *

I feel that the highest level of importance should be attached to the process of educating the young people who will, it is hoped, be faithful to the best of our traditions, be daring and energetic in their ability to bring about needed change, and, ultimately, be able to leave to their descendants a more highly developed sense of the potential of the human spirit. . . .

I would hope to move beyond the pettiness of rigid structure and arbitrary conduct to emerge with a community of individuals joined to each other in a commitment to the finest traditions of our cultural heritage. In an effort to maintain order in a spirit consistent with the philosophy, it is necessary to organize a structure based on reason, concern, and a sense of the common good. The community should be released from the tension of blind acceptance and the cynical fear-respect-contempt style of authority identification. The atmosphere is one in which excellence is rewarded, problems are dealt with fairly, and kindness is contagious—where the life of the school is a common endeavor. It is one that gives a sense of satisfaction, accomplishment, and comfort to everyone at every level of achievement and responsibility. . . .

* * *

It has not been a smooth or direct path by which I aspired to serve as an elementary school principal. . . . There have been roadblocks and detours along the way. I have also experienced and been involved with the best of educational thought and practice. The examples set by others, the inspiration, conviction, and inherent logic of certain writers, and my opportunities to collaborate with supportive practitioners are part of my journey. . . .

My most positive experiences have occurred in situations where I have taken initiative, worked closely and communicated readily with other professionals, and found myself in a school atmosphere where such behaviors were encouraged and given outlets for expression. Conversely, my frustrations have occurred in settings where some combination of these factors has been found lacking. . . .

First, I believe that, organizationally, I should work toward developing a sense of community as characteristic of the school setting. This would include not only teachers and students but parents and community members. Various forms of communication need to be developed, tried, and assessed. . . .

* * *

. . . Every child is curious about the world outside and inside. As educational theorists from Rousseau to Dewey have affirmed, that curiosity is the best motivation for and source of learning there is. And it must be honored by the teacher. Motivation is a very personal and ephemeral thing. No one can motivate anyone else. A teacher can create an environment, can stimulate, provoke, even inspire—but only you can motivate yourself. In fact, just as a freedom that is given is not a true freedom, because it can be taken away, so an education cannot be given; it must be taken for oneself. Giving without asking in return creates either passivity or indifference, attitudes destructive to both the learning process and the human personality. . . .

and intentions in the organized, concise, and disciplined manner required by the platform. Many were veterans of 15 years or more. Some suffered acute guilt pangs for practicing so long without systematically stating their beliefs. The writing process and the wrestling-with-self it brings can be the source of a great deal of both positive and negative emotional reaction.

Emotion is a deliberate component of platform writing and the course. Typically, we try to remain completely "rational"—that is, unemotional—in preparation courses and professional practice. (This is a universal "commandment" in organizational life with its roots in Model I assumptions.) In fact, emotions color our learning and most organizational decisions we make. I pay lots of attention to emotions, use several methods of decreasing the effects of negative emotions, and use both positive and negative emotions to move the reflective process forward.

More small group work follows platform writing. Students discuss in systematic fashion the emotions and thoughts experienced in wrestling and writing. These two categories, affective or "gut" responses and cognitive or "head" responses, are deliberately kept separate. I define behavior to include both emotion and thought. The platform process makes the definition concrete. Group members find they have shared much emotionally and cognitively while struggling and writing, and once this is in the open they feel more comfortable. And, inevitably, groups conclude that wrestling with themselves and then writing it down is an important and necessary step in self-understanding and professional growth. This discussion process is a powerful (if indirect and not recognized at the moment) source for building trust among the group. It is, in fact, a profoundly *professional* discussion, an act of sharing core professional values, issues, and concerns, an act too infrequently experienced by most educators.

Providing platform feedback. Another round of controlled discussion is conducted after group members have read each other's platforms and provided written *descriptive* feedback. Groups systematically discuss their affective and cognitive responses to reading and responding to the platforms of others before exchanging written feedback. Again, they discover shared emotions and thoughts in responding to each other. They often share the sense that responding to others was as or more difficult than writing their own platforms. They often experience an unspoken, deeply felt reverence for each other grounded in studying and attempting to reply to statements they know contain the distilled essence of colleagues' professional lives. Group trust grows tremendously in the process.

In providing platform feedback, I use the same systematic process I teach students to use with each other's work. The rationale for feedback is simply and *only* to provide the writer with a deeper understanding of what he or she has espoused in the platform. There are two tasks: (a) to note any logical inconsistencies among the parts of the document (fairly easy to do) and (b) to identify implicit assumptions that underlie the platform statements (extremely difficult to do). Detailed instructions are given in Figure 5.3.

The catch in giving feedback is that the reactor is required to provide only *descriptive,* not evaluative or prescriptive, feedback. Descriptive feedback is required because it is *helpful to the receiver* and less likely to cause a defensive reaction that distracts the receiver from thoughtful consideration of the platform itself (see Chapter 4). Providing descriptive feedback is a *very difficult process* because it goes against most of our socialization and the prevailing Model I norms and theory-in-use of most organizations. Providing a descriptive response is a truly *unnatural* act because it is grounded in Model II assumptions. But it is a very helpful and powerful gift to receive if one is focused on self-understanding and professional improvement.

Having responded to several hundred platforms, it still takes me an hour to provide really useful descriptive feedback for a two- to four-page statement. I work at responding to the particulars of each platform and at digging out assumptions lying below the surface. I find several theoretical frameworks from the literature to be useful identifiers of recurring patterns of platform assumptions. For example, an old framework is the differentiation between open and closed systems. Some platforms only mention issues and relationships within a classroom or building; these assume that schools are closed systems. Such platforms contain no mention of parent, community, state, or federal influences. Most students are familiar with the systems concepts, so a simple description, "The platform is based on closed systems assumptions," provides accurate feedback less likely to produce a defensive reaction and more likely to induce reflective attention than a prescription, "Schools are really open systems; you should include relationships with the environment in your platform." This point shows another reason for using an open-ended platform

Figure 5.3. Instructions for Responding to Colleagues' Platforms

You will provide feedback to the other members of your small group. The response will be descriptive rather than prescriptive. It will describe what *is,* what consensus would establish as reasonably factual. The feedback will not be used to say what the platform should be or why it is good or bad; such judgments are prescriptions. (We will discuss the difference between prescription and description thoroughly in class before giving feedback.)

There are two specific tasks with each platform:

(1) Check for internal, logical consistency. Can the various statements of the platform be espoused without contradicting each other? If there is consistency, simply state that you found it. If there are internal inconsistencies in logic, *describe* them, or, if there is a question without certainty on your part, raise the question.

(2) State explicitly any assumptions you see lying behind the various statements in the platform that are not specifically identified. This is not easy to do, but it is often very helpful to the writer. You will be helping to raise assumptions to the level of naming them so that the writer can examine them.

In addition to reading to make response, you will be reading the *content* and the *value* orientation of the platform. You will likely inherently agree or disagree with what the writer is saying—but do not respond to the writer with these prescriptive responses. Rather, use your prescriptive responses to the platforms of others as mirrors for understanding your own set of values and orientations. Take notes in your journal for *yourself* while you are working on descriptive comments to return to your peers. Sometimes a colleague will state something close to one of your own positions but use slightly different terms. It may be useful in helping you to see your own position in a slightly different way. You may also read a platform that contrasts considerably with yours, and you may want to argue with it. Rather than arguing with the colleague, take some notes in your journal about the realization. How does the tension you feel with another platform help to clarify your own position? Just try to turn arguments with others back upon yourself. Looked at in this way, you may surprise yourself and learn a good deal in the process.[a]

a. This is an example of awareness-raising through surprise or dilemma discussed in Chapter 2. Also, note the use of journal writing in this process.

format. What the writer produces in the platform is a truer indicator of his or her real thoughts and beliefs than if he or she is instructed to write about particular categories.

I find the following array of concepts useful in providing feedback about recurring patterns of assumptions: Sergiovanni (1980) divided educational purposes into two large categories—social utility and personal transcendence. The assumptions behind the four frames identified by Bolman and Deal (1991)—structural, human resource, political, and symbolic—are also useful and often revealing to writers. Some conceptions useful in identifying assumptions in the educational portions of the platform come from the dilemma framework of Berlak and Berlak (1981). Examples include the following: Do I engage the whole child or the child only as student? Do I control time or does the student have control of time? Do I treat knowledge as personal or as public? Do I treat knowledge as primarily content or process? Do I treat knowledge as given or problematical and constructed? Do I see motivation as extrinsic or intrinsic? Do I approach learning as holistic or molecular? Do I assume that learning is primarily social or individual? Do I tend to allocate resources differentially or equally? Do I stress a common culture or subgroup consciousness?

Facilitators will discover other useful categories.[2] Examples are offered only as suggestions and to illustrate one kind of descriptive feedback (e.g., "The platform contains both open and closed system assumptions and assumes that education is for the sole purpose of social utility") that writers have found useful in coming to deeper awareness of the larger assumptions underlying more specific platform statements.

One more issue arises in giving feedback. Because of our socialization and surrounding cultural and organizational norms (Model I, typically), we must *fight* to prevent ourselves from giving evaluative or prescriptive feedback of a positive or negative variety. ("I like what you say here; I believe it too" is a positive evaluative response.) I ask respondents to write in their journals the *evaluative* thoughts that come to mind while responding descriptively to others. The evaluations they would like to give—but are prevented from—when viewed differently are indicators of the respondent's own espoused theory triggered by reading another's platform. If I internally respond that I like or want to argue with a part of your platform, I can learn a great deal by looking back at my own platform to see whether my belief triggered by reading your platform shows up in my own work. In this way, responding to another's platform becomes a mirror for my own platform. Giving feedback to others becomes an exercise in reflection on my own espoused theory.

TESTING THE PLATFORM

Once the platform is written, the ways of engaging students in testing it—comparing it with observable behavior and eventually extrapolating the theory-in-use—are limited only by time, imagination, and willingness to take risks to learn. Over the years, I have varied the ways of probing for congruence and incongruence between the platform and actions as I experimented and reflected upon what happened and what I could learn of its effects on students. At Hofstra University, for example, I moved from a 2-night-a-week, 3½-weeks-in-January format to one evening and three all-day sessions in 3½ weeks, to four all-day sessions across most of a semester, to the current five all-day sessions across a semester. Changes came with more understanding of the importance of "intensity" in prolonged small group interaction and "reflective time" for writing, reading, thinking, and platform testing between class meetings. The current scheduling provides enough intensity for groups to move beyond a superficial level to real trust building and the 3 weeks between sessions allow time for personal reflection through wrestling with ideas, writing, and reading.

Using role plays. Because my students are diverse, I use contrived experiences, mostly role plays, to generate public behavior for analysis in the testing phase of the platform sequence. Role plays vary from pairs working simultaneously to large groups playing before the rest of the class as audience. In most cases, I ask players to construct miniplatforms (see Chapter 4) or brief statements of their

Figure 5.4. Examples of Supervisory Situations Adapted From Johnston (1985)

In each of the following situations, put yourself into the role of a supervisor that makes sense to you in your particular situation. It may be the role of building principal or assistant principal, department chairperson, or some kind of district supervisor.

1. A teacher has been late to school and to homeroom. The situation first came to your attention when you observed students standing by the classroom doorway after the last bell had rung. You questioned the students and discovered that there was a pattern to the teacher's late arrival. You have left a note in the teacher's mailbox requesting that he or she see you after school. In the current situation, that teacher has just arrived.

2. You are a supervisor who is about to meet with a teacher at the end of the teacher's second year of teaching. If the teacher continues in the same pattern for the third year, it is your judgment that tenure should not be granted, and you will be party to the decision. You think there is potential for a good teacher here, but there are also problems currently as you see it: student physical movement around the classroom unrelated to learning activities, student conversation in large amounts not related to learning activities, about one third to one half of the stated learning goals are not met in a typical lesson.

intentions and methods (espoused theory). The content of the role play matters less than its ability to engage students, to have them "get lost" in the action, so their behaviors are more authentic than "play acting." Two examples are shown in Figure 5.4.

Christine Johnston (1985) developed supervisory scenarios for her dissertation. I converted them to role play setups with a teacher and a supervisor (see Figure 5.4).

I use these role plays as an exercise in facilitating descriptive feedback—a requirement given to the student playing the supervisor. The supervisor writes down what he or she hopes to accomplish in the role play. The play is then undertaken. At completion, actors exchange *only* descriptive feedback (to facilitate nondefensive communication as explained earlier). The supervisor reads the miniplatform and then tells the supervisee what he or she thinks has been accomplished. The supervisee then describes how he or she felt, what he or she is going to do as a result of the interchange, and the accuracy of the supervisor's description of events and outcomes. When it works well, the supervisee receives the kind of crucial performance feedback typically withheld in organizations—real data on the effects of his or her actions. The actors may then replay the scenario with the same actors playing the same parts to allow the supervisor to experiment with different behaviors (i.e., the experiential learning process discussed in Chapter 2), swap roles and play the same role play again, or move on to a different scenario. I ask players to take notes in their journals and to compare or test the miniplatforms and the actions generated during the role plays against their platforms.

For one large group role play, I use an old yet powerful case from the University Council for Educational Administration materials. The scenario concerns a new principal who must confront a 40-year veteran teacher in the school passed over for the principalship. She has a history of unacceptable behaviors in seeking to become a principal and an assistant superintendent who is out to get her and who has essentially "set up" the new principal to do his or her dirty work. The situation is a powerful demonstration of the "conspiracy of silence": The veteran teacher has never been told what she is doing wrong. The scene opens with the teacher bursting in to see the principal about the news in the grapevine that she has just been taken off the districtwide curriculum committee on which she is expert and upon which her self-esteem rests.

I typically have between four and five volunteer pairs play the teacher and principal parts. Each student in the room writes a miniplatform for each role before the action begins. We play the pairs serially with no comment in between. Typically, both teacher and principal play the roles in ways distinct from other pairs; there is usually considerable variety. The most important part is debriefing; sufficient time must be allocated or the impact is lost. I debrief in a controlled and descriptive way. The principals state their miniplatforms; I write them on the board. Teachers' intentions are also recorded. Then I go back and ask the principals for success estimates and if necessary to indicate where they succeeded and where they failed. I ask for their estimates of the teachers' success as well. Teachers then give their success and failure perceptions. Everything is descriptive. No one is allowed to say things like the following: "I think you should have . . ." or "It would have been better if you had . . .".

Both players get information on performance and results of their actions in a straightforward way seldom available in real situations. Probing may continue further with players asking for more detailed descriptions and clarifications. Continued probing may be done in public or private. Recently, I have tape-recorded each separate run-through of the role play and given this complete data record to the individual playing the principal role. She or he may then take it home for careful and private analysis. Regardless of how far beyond basic feedback the role plays are pushed, all observers see multiple approaches and their results. The crucial issue is to keep everything descriptive. That way, each individual has much to reflect upon and must come to her or his own conclusions. Keeping the talk descriptive "protects" the players to a large degree and prevents the class from "ganging up" on a player by telling him or her "how to do it better." It keeps defensiveness to a minimum and encourages all to focus on the relationship between behaviors and platforms, whether congruent or incongruent.

Role plays can be powerful devices for sparking reflective activity, deepening the level of trust, demonstrating the importance and power of providing actors with descriptive feedback about their behaviors, motivating students to take reasonable risks in other settings to generate behavioral data, and demonstrating how typical Model I organizational norms must be set aside for real learning about behavior and its effects to occur. As facilitator, I work very hard in role plays at "protecting" actors by keeping the feedback descriptive, focusing data on comparing the espoused with action, and encouraging spectators to make vicarious use of the action and feedback. Because everyone has at least developed an espoused position and seen the results of trying to enact espousals, all have something substantial to reflect about, write about in journals, and perhaps debrief in groups later. Everyone has behavioral data from which to attempt to construct theories-in-use, their own and others'. I use all sorts of "contrived" situations to generate fairly authentic and public behavior. Role plays can be a powerful vehicle for stimulating reflection if done well—but they can produce trust-defeating embarrassment if done poorly.

Facilitating a role play such as the principal/teacher scenario described above is always emotionally draining for me. I am frequently exhausted after the all-day sessions of "The Reflective Administrator" course. Role plays, like all reflective practice learning experiences that pack a real possibility for deep learning, are open ended. Facilitating them is always an exercise in faith surrounded by a fog of ambiguity. Very seldom, in my experience, do they become negative to the point of being destructive—but the possibility is always there. Should real illness develop, the best antidote is probably more *description,* more valid information, and using the very problem itself as a basis for reflection. This paragraph is simply one more message to those who would be facilitators that it is a difficult, serious, and sometimes quite uncomfortable role, but one that must be taken for others to learn by engaging in the process of reflection itself.

Using other means. Writing case records under the format developed by Silver (1986) and modified by Osterman (1991) is another method of focusing on behavior and looking for congruency or discrepancy between the espoused and enacted (see Chapter 4). Case records focus on past rather than contemporary actions, but they can be powerful sources for reflection. I have students develop several cases and share them in small groups. In learning to reflect, the critical issue is not the facts of the case, the resolution worked out, or a hypothetically better approach. Rather, it is the *process* of reflecting on past behavior, assessing it in relationship to one's platform, and carrying this forward to test again in new situations.

Autobiographical writing is another means of focusing on the relationship between intentions and actions (see Chapter 4). Such work is often useful in cutting to the core of one's theory-in-use and the cultural assumptions behind it. Writing about almost any important experience as a student, teacher, or administrator may spark important insight. Issues such as power, authority, and control are important foci for autobiographical work. (Miller's [1990a] extensive work on a teacher researcher group demonstrates the importance of this mode of generating data on behavior and understanding its assumptional roots.) This writing may also be important grist for small group discussion. I find that students often discover common themes because their experiences arise from a relatively consistent school culture. They sometimes push far enough to see important organizational influences and constraints that need to be challenged or restructured if they are to achieve espoused intentions.

Journal keeping is another important reflective device (see Chapter 4). Students keep a journal of important insights and descriptions of what they do. I often do "stop action" sequences in the course. At the end of an activity such as a role play or discussion—or sometimes in the middle of one—I stop them; they take out their journals and write their reflections. They record miniplatforms in journals when we do role plays. I encourage frequent entries about their reading and their daily actions. I ask them to keep records of their own self-developed means of comparing behavior with their platforms. There is, in addition to the uses I make of journals, an entire literature on various types of journal keeping for different purposes (Fulwiler, 1987; Holly, 1989; Progoff, 1975; Roderich, 1986). I try to use journal writing as a means to focus attention on congruities and discrepancies between the espoused platform and actual behaviors and as a source for the extrapolation of one's theory-in-use.

Instruments are another way of focusing attention on one's own behavior. Though I use a number of these, the one I find most powerful as a stimulator of reflection is the Myers-Briggs Type Indicator (Myers & McCaulley, 1985). It provides feedback on the individual's typical modes of perceiving, making sense of data, and coming to decisions. Students take this instrument before coming to the first class; I use it along with other data (sex type, role, experience, schooling level, academic program) in creating small groups. I purposely make diverse groups so all members are able to garner feedback and perceptions from individuals who see the world with different lenses. One example is introversion and extroversion as technically defined through this instrument. Introverts are in the minority (25% in the general population) and process data very differently than extroverts. I make sure there is at least one introvert in each group and focus attention on the differences between the two orientations. Students typically use such feedback to understand themselves and to understand why some individuals act quite differently in, for example, formal meetings. Most students find instruments in general, and the Myers-Briggs in particular, helpful in examining their own behaviors. They often use such terms as "scary" and "uncanny" to describe the accuracy they perceive in the self-descriptions they receive from the Myers-Briggs feedback.

Another useful and fun means of gathering descriptive feedback on behavior is creating metaphors. Toward the end of the course, each individual develops a metaphor symbolizing his or her group and group members, including the creator, to be shared with the others. These symbolic devices provide another set of lenses through which behaviors exhibited in the group's life may be described. This interpretive framework often results in highlighting perceptions differing from straight behavioral description, yet the perceptions remain descriptive.

I encourage students to be inventive and assertive in finding ways of testing their platforms in the workplace. Means for doing this include video- or audiotaping, examining memos and other written materials, keeping logs of activities, keeping detailed journals, shadowing each other, seeking feedback from other sources where safe enough, and writing additional case records. The small groups often "jell" into very useful, supportive environments for members to receive the kinds of information about their behaviors they do not get elsewhere. I encourage them to consult each other on the phone about work issues, to hold additional meetings during the course, and to continue to work together after the course.

In the past, I have asked students to write a short paper on the workplace constraints they meet in attempting to realize their platforms. It helps them to focus on the elements of their environments they need to change so as to exercise their platforms. Sharing these papers may solidify understanding of the kinds of structures, norms, and cultures that support or oppose reflective practice. Those in leadership positions may come to a better understanding of the sorts of changes and buffering they need to work on to create an environment safe enough for their subordinates to try reflection.

EVIDENCE OF COURSE EFFECTS

As a new professor more than a dozen years ago, I began to develop and use reflective content in administrative preparation after reading Argyris and Schon (1974) and finding a resonant cord deep within me. I was, at the time, in a personal struggle over the contents of legitimate administrative preparation, over whether what I had been doing had any real value in helping my students to improve education for children. I was confronting the ontological question. This was before reflection was popular.

Being relatively alone in the field, I was sustained by my faith in what I was doing and buoyed up by reports from students who said it was a valuable—some went as far as to say "indispensable"—part of their education. So I worked with my own observations and anecdotal reports from my students. In 1989, I formalized assessment by surveying all the students I had had in reflection courses at Rutgers and Hofstra Universities. The result was an academic paper (Kottkamp, 1990b). Presented here in capsule form are the findings from this survey study. One open-ended survey is probably not the best mode for understanding the questions I am asking, but the results are very encouraging.

I posed three questions for the study:

1. What was the value of the reflection course in comparison to other courses in the administrative preparation program?
2. Did the experience of developing and testing a platform for discrepancies with professional action have real short and long term effects on professional practice and personal life?
3. Did students adapt and apply reflection and discrepancy identification to other groups or individuals? (Kottkamp, 1990b, p. 4)

Respondents rated the "value or usefulness of the platform development and testing sequence for [their] own professional practice" in comparison with other required administrative courses (e.g., organizational theory, supervision, school law, curriculum, principalship). In all cases, former students ranked reflection more important than the others, though not tremendously so.

The more interesting impact data, however, came from the open-ended essay responses to the second and third questions. I analyzed these into two categories: (a) perceived real changes in professional practice (or personal life) and (b) applications, adaptations, and instruction of others in skills learned from the platform writing and testing sequence. Table 5.1 shows subcategories of responses for each large question and the percentages of individuals who responded to each category.

Direct Effects on Professional Practice and Life Beyond Work

Increased general reflectivity, introspection, and enhanced self-understanding. One third of the respondents reported continuing effects on professional practice from the process of reflection, introspection, self-monitoring, examination of beliefs, values, and discrepancy finding between intention and action. Examples included standing outside of yourself and observing, introspection on interpersonal problems, knowing where you stand, honest assessment of your own teaching, greater awareness of your own views and greater ability to work for them or reconsider them, thinking more before acting and understanding the importance of getting the big picture, providing professional focus, increased awareness of how words and actions represent character and conviction, and how words and deeds often do not convey what is believed or intended.

Reflection became a pervasive operational mode, a guide to action. For these respondents, reflection became an important, if not determining, guide for action. They reported important perspective changes; their basic assumptions had been affected and changed. This group reported that the reflection experiences helped to guide and validate actions, increased their ability to communicate philosophy and expectations clearly, allowed them to temper their actions by observing themselves as an outside party, and helped them to distinguish between "constants" and the ebb and flow of societal demands on education. Some used the platform to invoke a state of discomfort when

TABLE 5.1
Open-Ended Responses to How Reflection Affected
Professional Practice

Responses	Percentage
Real Changes in Professional Practice or Personal Life:	
No effect or no data given	15
Increased general reflectivity, introspection, and enhanced self-understanding	36
Reflection became a pervasive operational mode, a guide to action	13
Effects on specific areas of action	34
Insights leading to broad perspective shift	6
Increased confidence and commitment	22
Help with job searches and decisions	31
Important effects on personal life	12
Useful in developing dissertation research problems	4
Application of Platform and Reflective Means to Others:	
Did not apply reflection to others or no data	42
Applications to supervision and discrepancy finding	14
Applications to using descriptive communication	8
Applications to journal writing	9
Applications to teaching superiors	5
Teaching the platform writing sequence to others	4
Applications to parents	4
Applications to students	6
Miscellaneous applications	16

NOTE: Percentages add up to more than 100% because some individuals gave answers in several categories.

they forgot to exercise choice in their behaviors. A central office special education supervisor, for example, commented:

> Inevitably, I ask myself what is it I want to accomplish, and the answer bounces back to my original platform statements. I realize that now due to this current exercise [answering the survey] . . . I continuously seek to encourage teachers in examining their purposes, actions, conflicts. The approach [reflective practice] has

helped me develop the strongest department in the district. "We" are described as *good teachers,* good people, possessing camaraderie, supportive, etc. We are also the department that "collaborates" with all our colleagues most effectively. Special Education has become the tail that wags the dog. . . . We value kids! Everyone knows that!

Effects on specific areas of action. One third of the individuals answered in this category, but many named more than one area. Important areas included greater awareness and openness to ideas, views, and beliefs of others with resulting improvement of relationships and meetings; greater attention to the supervisee's view and intention in supervisory situations; more careful monitoring of their own beliefs during action; more use of descriptive communication in helping others to examine their behaviors; improved decision making because of more perspectives being taken into account; shifted perspective toward students from control to leadership; greater willingness to stand up for their convictions; improved teaching through sharing personal philosophy with students who better understood teacher intentions and assignments; increased policy decisions based on the platform; and curriculum changed to make intentions and outcomes congruent. A state department educator commented on the effect the course had on her teaching at that time:

It was very helpful to have the opportunity to examine in depth the beliefs under which I had been operating up to that time. The primary result was a dramatic change in the ways I controlled students [becoming much more positive, much less punitive].

A district mathematics supervisor said:

Argyris and Schon left an indelible impression on my professional self. I frequently reflect upon my own "congruence" or lack thereof when I question my effectiveness as Supervisor of Mathematics. I must confess that I am reminded of the difference between one's espoused theory and theory-in-use because I observe so much of it when I observe classes. I am convinced that most teachers have two scripts—one which drives their discussions, e.g. in the faculty room or at the department meeting—the other which drives their behavior in the classroom. This gap makes it difficult for a supervisor to have an effect on teachers.

Insights leading to broad perspective shifts. Respondents named specific course insights that led to major perspective shifts. One described increased "sensitivity" to others with differing beliefs resulting from intense small group work with people having varying platforms. Another wrote of insight into "ownership," of taking different interests and interpersonal relationships into account rather than simply imposing ideas through power. A counselor described an increased understanding of administrative actions that may not fit teachers' perspectives but really may be in the interest of the children. Another wrote of a shift in view to this one: "You *can* beat city hall!" and a commitment to making an impact congruent with his own values. Another teacher described a broad perspective change:

> The real change is within me. I stopped thinking and behaving as a teacher. I started to act as a leader. It was as if I had stepped outside of myself and "saw" through a long-term, wide angle lens. . . . My classroom behavior changed. I stopped thinking "control" and started to think "leadership . . ." As a result of the course, my classroom behavior changed. Students *vote* on topics *we* as a class will learn. Students know that they are being heard and heeded. It made a tremendous difference in their classroom behavior. . . . Reflective feedback is used at the end of every major unit. . . . I use "I statements" in class. . . . I have helped department members articulate and clarify their platforms via descriptive feedback. . . . I learned to list and value *any* feedback a student gives me. . . . I believe the platform is the most singularly powerful tool available to any administrator.

Increased confidence and commitment. A quarter of the former students used terms like increased "confidence," "inner strength," "standing up for what I believe," "encouragement of personal commitment to professional conduct," "security in having mentally double-checked that I was looking at the total concept," "determination to reach goals," "growth . . . feel good about myself." Others said: "chance to reassess and reaffirm convictions," "verification of beliefs and practices," "a therapeutic and authentication experience," "real change within me from thinking/behaving as a teacher to feeling/acting as a leader." A central office supervisor noted: "The platform 'effort' has often provided the confidence I needed to carry through on a plan. I knew the curricular approach was right, for example. . . . It was valid for kids—damn the politics!" These strong, positive, emotionally laden words used to describe personal changes in professional practice indicate the process touched important issues for these individuals.

Help with job searches and decisions. One third indicated the course helped with job searches and decisions. The course helped with the interview process: "became more relaxed and in tune with my own model of educational needs," "more articulate about what you stand for," "more focused in career direction," "more specific in interviews," "helped to be positively received," and "came across more sure of myself because of self-knowledge." There were results beyond interviews. Several noted an "increased view of the scope of future possibilities" or "a decision to move from the classroom to a more responsible position matching my goals and needs." Several wrote of rejecting job offers because they did not match espoused theories and self-knowledge; each of these indicated a positive personal outcome from the decision.

Effects on personal life. A small number reported effects of the reflective experience beyond work. One wrote of "honest assessment of personal relationships with all those whose lives intertwine with mine—professional, casual and intimate." Another described a "wider perspective on options . . . no longer either/or but possibly this . . . or perhaps that." Another wrote of the helpfulness of descriptive feedback in "dealing with a teenage daughter who requires constant interactive support and guidance." One reported personal life improvement "because I felt better about myself . . . got married and felt the need to improve and change the way I view people and the way I teach." Several doctoral students described how the reflection course had helped them to complete dissertations. The most gripping statement concerned confronting cancer at age 39. Her reflective experience aided with "awareness of values and priorities that helped me to devise a plan for survival." The plan included dropping administrative aspirations, pulling back from a perfectionistic, "all A's" orientation, and a realization that her primary focus was to be a good teacher and mother.

Application of Reflection to Others

Almost three fifths of survey respondents indicated applying the platform sequence, reflective means, or skills to others in their workplaces. Individuals in quite different administrative roles reported using and instructing their subordinates in finding discrepancies between intention and action as a means of improving performance. Many indicated the value of using descriptive feedback.

A state-level staff developer, a professor, a counselor/consultant, and a principal indicated using journals as vehicles in teaching others to reflect. Several reports indicated the effect of increasing participation in decision making. Areas included curriculum, policy, program reorganization and implementation, and planning.

One teacher explained reflective concepts to an administrator who was both "shocked and pleased" to learn of the means. A chairperson shared the platform idea with a new administrator from a very closed system who was in conflict with staff. He became more open to suggestions, appreciative of staff, more trusting, and better liked. Chairpersons and principals reported adopting the platform sequence as a base for teacher supervision, and a central administrator, as a means for working with interns. A high school principal taught the process to his assistants and was amazed at the discrepancies they uncovered together. An assistant principal created a reflective parenting workshop. Teachers reported using reflective means in parent meetings.

Some of the most creative and heartening applications of reflective means came in adaptations to work with students. One high school teacher described having students write their own platforms and then test them against their performance. Discrepancy finding was especially potent with average and below average students. A

fourth-grade teacher explained how telling the students *her* platform—explaining "why" to them through telling them her philosophy of education—resulted in a much higher degree of acceptance
of assignments and requests. A teacher learning consultant described
applications to at-risk, disaffected students for solving their own
problems, including journal writing, communication exercises, and
scenarios moving them toward or away from attaining their goals.
These means helped to give them "some power and clarity they had
given up on."

Meanings

On the whole, former students perceived positive and continuing
effects of the platform sequence on their professional practices and,
to a lesser degree, on their personal lives: 85% perceived direct influence on their own practice, while 58% described applications
including others. There was no negative response, only silence or statement of no effect. The language describing personal use of reflection
and reflective skills was personal, powerful, testimonial, emotional,
normative, at times passionate. Many of the responses had a ring of
"believers" excited about an approach to professional work that
was meaningful, understandable, and practical. There were even
reports going beyond social science concepts such as "perspective
change" to what seemed to be "conversion experiences." The responses were about important and personal things, about very personal meanings.

These former students reported a greater usefulness of the platform writing and testing sequence for their own professional practice
than from other required administration courses. Unlike courses that
focus on theories or rules of thumb about how things work "out there"
in the world, the meaning and utility of reflection probably stems
from its uniqueness in making the student thinker/actor the central
focus of the experience. (Field internships have the *potential* for a
similar focus, but participants often are focused on figuring out how
the successful mentor acts and then attempting to "copy" his or her
behavior. This is very different than focusing primarily on intention/

action discrepancies for the self.) The platform sequence is an intensely personal experience.

Reading the survey responses reaffirmed the central and critical position of the *educational* foundation for the administrative platform. There is almost universal admission among practicing educators of never having systematically inquired into their own belief systems in a disciplined way requiring a product that then can be carefully examined, modified, and used over the years to come. Numerous self-identified "naturally introspective" individuals indicated that it was important to have a formal requirement that "forced" them to produce what they would probably not have accomplished on their own.

I suspect that another reason beyond the personal focus for the platform receiving higher utility scores than other administrative courses was its very specific *educational* focus. Few traditional administration courses deal with core classroom educational issues. This course makes the individual's educational values and beliefs central. Further, a significant proportion of teachers complete administrative certification programs but remain in classrooms. The platform sequence may provide the greatest utility for many graduates precisely because it focuses on issues, meanings, and actions that have the classroom as their locus. The platform development and testing sequence provides both immediate utility and future potential for almost all students.

The analytical description of the course provides a broad overview of its impact and utility but misses some of the power, passion, and depth of more full personal accounts. I asked four recent students who appeared to have benefited from the experience to write personal statements or testimonials and have chosen to end this chapter with slightly edited versions of two of them. They make the meaning of reflective practice come alive in vivid ways.

Liz

> I have just closed my first year . . . as chairperson. Much of this year's meaning is the direct result of my work in a reflective practice framework.

. . . I was so ripe for this course; much of my growth work had been on a personal level. This course gave me the invaluable opportunity to bridge the gaps between the personal Liz and the professional Liz. Without the course, I'm not sure I would have made it through the past year.

The most powerful tool I gained was developing my "espoused theory." It became my center and along with my desire for "follow through" formed the strength I needed to perform. My dysfunctional background as well as my natural tendencies have always dictated a need to be liked. This problem caused me to be all over the place at decision time or when the tough stuff arose. All my efforts to detach from this behavior had only gotten me so far. It was the framework of Argyris's "espoused theory" as opposed to "theory-in-use" that gave me the tools, the strength, and the power I needed to do the hard stuff.

I spent the semester examining my espoused theories and developing my theory-in-use. It was the most productive time I've ever spent. (I even managed finally to reduce it to three words.) Out of it came my focus for this year; every time there was a decision to make or a behavior to evaluate, I used my espoused theory as my ruler. For the most part my actions remained true to what I believed, and it felt so good. I have become a better teacher and a good administrator because of it. I had to supervise ten 35-plus-year industrial arts teachers who refused to shift toward the new technology emphasis. It was a male-phobic, need-to-be-liked person's nightmare. Daily I had to give feedback about unacceptable or inappropriate behavior, lack of student supervision, poor instructional techniques, lack of parental follow-up . . . and the list goes on. My ability to give feedback came from the security I felt by measuring what I needed to do against what I believed. The power of that one task of developing a theory-in-use was incredible. I felt integrated for the first time in my career.

There were two other significant tools for growth that I acquired as the result of the reflective practice course. One was the notion that I could make meaning from sharing with others, that I could reflect out loud and gain incredible insights from that process. I have always been introspective. Alone, though, I am limited to sifting through stuff from my own perspective. I never felt truly secure enough to reflect in a group. I always shared in group situations—but only things I had long ago resolved and made meaning from. Part of learning to reflect in a group necessitated growing to a level of personal security to allow it to happen. Fortunately I had that prior to the course. All I needed was introduction to reflecting in a group, and the course did that. . . .

I became so excited about this process that I vowed to form a group to continue group reflection when the course ended. It was this newly created group that so often facilitated for me the making of meaning regarding all the stuff that hits me in this new job. I remember the session where I was so anxious and angry. I was defining tasks that had to be done (via my ruler) and was doing them, yet I was generally unsuccessful in altering behavior, and all I could seem to do at that point was blame the system. It was only through sharing and reflecting with the group that the pattern emerged and the problem became a concept I could understand: I had been doing much of my communication in writing. Writing enabled me to do the task, but I was sacrificing tangible tools at hand by not approaching people face-to-face. The group also helped me to see why I was making the choice to communicate in this way, despite the fact that I had not started out that way. It was a powerful discovery and really helped me leap past the anger and move toward a new challenge of learning to deal face-to-face. It brought my focus back to "what I could do" and away from "what I can't change at the moment."

The third significant tool from the course was descriptive feedback. This concept is probably the reason that the Assistant Superintendent for Personnel approached me last week and told me that I "write the best observations she has seen in 22 years as head of personnel." It is a concept I struggle with daily; I'm often interspersing prescriptive with descriptive feedback, but I continue to strive to become better at being descriptive in the information I give to others.

My goal is to be the best administrator I can be, not just an administrator. I can only achieve this goal as it unfolds on a day-to-day basis if I use my tools of reflection. It is that simple for me.

Maryann

The power of reflection . . . unfolded as I moved from being a student to a practitioner. I have been able to make great use of time spent with my constituents and able to ensure that my actions and goals are in accordance. For me, it is ongoing self-evaluation. Reflection frees me to do many things because I am "mucking through stuff" on a continuous basis. Prior to being fairly well integrated in this process, I found well spread out peaks (meaningful stuff) and valleys (not meaningful stuff) in my day-to-day actions. Nowadays, I find more peaks.

You introduced me to reflection, and [three] things assisted in making it a realistic piece of my repertoire . . . knowledge of my "type" on the Myers-Briggs Type Indicator . . . Bolman and Deal's frames for interpreting actions in organizations . . . showed me I could look at things from a perspective other than my own . . . Barry Jentz's . . . how to give negative information to people in a way that it can be heard. I came away from these experiences with a keen awareness of my tendency to react instead of respond and of my tendency to think out loud. I went into my new job as assistant principal wanting to be responsive to the needs of school community members, but knowing I would not always have the luxury to "talk it out." I went in with the notion of using interactions among people as a vehicle to reflect on what is operating when people give each other information. I also went to work for a principal who looks for others' interpretations of situations and facilitates reflecting on daily occurrences. I moved my stance from being the "person with the answer" to being a facilitator charged with enabling people to do a variety of things.

About three weeks into my position, I realized I viewed administration as a process. . . . Work was exhausting. I literally came home at night and "replayed the tape" to analyze it (or attempt to do so) and would fall asleep by 9:00. I found I could talk things out at home and with the other assistants and the principal. But then came February.

The fiscal picture on Long Island . . . was murky with impending sharp reductions in state aid. I was told by the superintendent's office that, although my performance was positive, I would very possibly be out of a job. Upper-level administrators would assist me where possible, but I was advised to protect myself by applying for other positions. I was devastated.

In retrospect, the experience of the next few months was growth inducing. I was even aware of it at the time because I was studious in my adherence to responding to information before me and *not* reacting emotionally to my fears or concerns. On the job, I was able to exceed the standards of my building and my own standards. I not only did the routine work, but took on some difficult issues with kids, parents, and staff. I added a new portion to my mental loop. Aware of my anger, I worked hard at looking at my own motivation for doing things. This was purely a means of ensuring that I was not acting out of anger, not making someone else feel miserable in order to have something to focus on.

I applied for chair of special education in another district and was offered the job. The district wanted a commitment in two weeks. The picture in my own district was no clearer. I had a choice between a step-backwards position and a job I loved that might evaporate. My immediate reaction, based on fear (mortgage payments and homelessness), was to take the job in hand. I established two goals for the decision. First, I would take the full time allotted. Second, I would seek all possible additional information in my district.

In this process, . . . I had to recognize the emotional stuff I was feeling in order to deal with the decision. Once I did that, I was able to focus on obtaining and processing information. I spent no time directing my anger toward others—I had no idea how useful that could be as a means of time management! It allowed me to do all the things . . . in my job. It was a revelation that I could be under such tremendous pressure and not retreat— literally *or* figuratively. I also learned I had the ability to make decisions that were not reactions to fear but based on information and identifying the choice which best fit my goals. I found strength in the process and took a large gamble in turning down the job. It was a crossroad decision for me, one I made well.

Taking a reflective approach toward people had a great impact on my professional life and personal side as well. It really helped me to get through the employment crisis. I'm not sure which is the chicken and which the egg, but I have grown a great deal since I integrated reflection into my orientation.

NOTES

1. See Kottkamp (1982, 1990b) for more complete descriptions of the courses at various times during their evolution.

2. Michael O'Loughlin, a Hofstra colleague, uses other categories in working with preservice teacher education students.

6 A Reflective Approach to Principal Renewal

In 1990, the Council of Supervisors and Administrators and the New York City Board of Education established provisions for involuntary transfer of principals.[1] Those principals who were not performing effectively in their positions and might benefit from a skill building program would be released from their positions for a full semester to participate in a full-time professional development program consisting of an individualized plan of services designed to address their specific strengths and deficits and drawing on a wide range of participatory programs and activities.

In August 1990, Bank Street College of Education was selected by the NYC Board of Education to develop and operate the Professional Development Center (PDC) and the Hofstra University School of Education was invited to participate. Out of the initial planning sessions grew a plan for four strands of activities: (a) school residencies with principal partners, effective leaders in schools with exemplary programs; (b) support activities including seminars, workshops, conferences, individualized reading, and school visitations;

(c) mentoring and advising by retired principals and Bank Street faculty and staff; and (d) a reflective practice seminar.

Of the 20 principals initially assigned to the Professional Development Center, 17 chose to retire, so, in September, 3 secondary school principals—John, Sara, and Abby—entered what was known in the ranks as "The Gulag" or "The Principals' Prison." Following an individualized assessment, they began their work. For 3 to 4 days a week, the principals—all members of minority groups and all senior administrators with more than 25 years of experience—worked in schools with their principal partners. They also attended seminars, workshops, and conferences offered by other universities, schools, and private corporations; visited other schools—including some in Dade County—to observe exemplary schools and programs; and met with mentors and advisers to discuss their experiences. In addition, from October through December of that year, the principals met at Hofstra University for a weekly half-day seminar. This chapter describes the seminar itself and the experiences of the participants and the facilitator within the context of the Professional Development Center program.

THE REFLECTIVE PRACTICE SEMINAR

Objectives

Quite clearly, the purpose of this program was to create behavioral change. Consistent with the philosophy of learning outlined in Chapter 2, the intent was to provide an experience that would enable these principals (a) to identify and assess the theories-in-use that shape their administrative behavior, (b) to develop a new conceptual framework for leadership, and (c) to begin to integrate these new ideas and behaviors into their professional practice prior to their return to the principalship. An important related objective was to enable the principals to develop communication skills that facilitate collaboration and conflict resolution.

Activities

Consistent with the guidelines discussed in earlier chapters, I intended the reflective practice seminar to be a secure environment, a laboratory where the principals could examine their ideas or theories about leadership openly and freely and experiment with new ideas and new ways of acting.

Beginning the inquiry: Experience. The first session opened with a brief introduction to reflective practice stressing how practice is often divergent from intent and the importance of examining practice, and specifically problems of practice, as a means of improvement. For the remainder of the session, we talked about their principalships and the recent events that had shaken their sense of professional competence and self-esteem. Sara was threatened with formal dismissal after a student disturbance erupted; Abby had been the center of a highly politicized controversy in the school and district. After a long, quiet career, John volunteered to take over a troubled school. Attempting to address the problems, he found himself caught between conflicting expectations of teachers and central administration. Problems escalated and he agreed to leave the position and enter the PDC. We talked about their experiences and tried to develop a reflective perspective: What were the events that led to the problem? What had they done to contribute to the problem? What could they have done that might have helped? We talked about the criteria that others—the central office, teachers, parents—used to judge their performance and about their performance relative to those criteria. At this point, I shifted the conversation from a discussion of what the principal is expected to do to what they as principals wanted to accomplish and the relationship between the two sets of expectations. From then on, we focused on their personal goals and objectives and their effectiveness in realizing their own visions of leadership.

As another means of developing the reflective perspective, I asked each principal to define her or his own agenda for the balance of the course: In what areas did they feel weak? What were their problem spots? Where did they most feel the need for improvement? In retrospect, we all agreed that this was an important activity; for them to take control of their professional growth and to assume responsibility for their own learning, they needed to establish their own agenda. At the end of the course, Abby remarked that, if I had tried to control the agenda, "giving [them] a paper to write and articles to read, [she] probably would have told [me] to go to hell." From their perspective, being able "to create the guidelines within the group, to create the subject, the idea you were going to focus on" made the program. They described how deciding what their concerns were, why they were in the program, and having to get the answers from themselves and from the others in the group helped them to assume personal responsibility for their learning and to begin to think about what they could get out of the program.

While the principals' provided the content, I provided the conceptual and theoretical framework. Because of my personal belief that Model II assumptions and behavior are closely linked both to reflective practice and to organizational and leader effectiveness, the seminar was grounded in Argyris and Schon's formulation of Model I/Model II (see Chapter 3). Over the next few weeks, then, we focused on problems of practice emerging from their own experience to accomplish two objectives: (a) to explore the principals' underlying assumptions (theories-in-use) about leadership and control and (b) to develop Model II communication skills, specifically skills of listening and descriptive feedback. As the principals shared their experience, they were also developing a critical awareness of their own theories-in-use and their patterns of communication and interaction, and developing skills in reflective listening and descriptive feedback.

Observation and analysis. Through a number of techniques outlined in Chapter 4, the principals brought their experiences into the classroom for observation and analysis. Initially, they wrote case records and told stories about incidents in their schools that had been troublesome for them. The process of writing and narration in itself helps to establish the detached stance that facilitates observation and reflection.

Role plays also proved to be very effective in stimulating reflection. The case records and narrative incident reports provided the material for the role plays. Following a discussion of the case to clarify the facts and to raise questions, the principals would reenact the situation. Following each role play, the participants described their own feelings and reactions and then received feedback from the other participants and observers.

With feedback in hand, it was then possible to analyze the situation as a means of identifying the underlying theory-in-use and also to test the effectiveness of that theory: Why did they act as they had? What were they thinking? What was the rationale? Did the actions lead to the intended outcomes? In one session, for example, when we were discussing how principals exercise leadership and, specifically, how they work with teachers, two of the principals described situations in which they had been unsuccessful in getting teachers involved in a proposed change. In one situation, the principal was trying to introduce cooperative learning; in the other, site-based management. We then role played a meeting in which the principals met with teachers to introduce the idea. This exercise had a dual effect. Although in earlier discussions the principals had not addressed teacher needs or feelings, in the role play, they had no difficulty expressing the anger and frustration that teachers feel when they have little control. As a result of playing the teacher's role, they had the opportunity to experience that anger and frustration firsthand. In that exercise, they also experienced their own resistance to sharing authority with the teachers and, with the feedback from the other participants, were able to see how their actions created anger and resistance rather than interest and support.

Through this activity, the principals developed a level of empathy with teachers that had not been evident in earlier discussions. They also became more critically aware of their own administrative behavior and dissatisfied with the impact of their strategies on others. Sara, for example, who was very supportive of shared decision making, said that, while she had never thought of herself as controlling, she could now see that she was. All found that their beliefs about the best way to introduce change in schools needed to be reexamined.

Reconceptualization and experimentation. Once dissatisfaction had been aroused, the principals were more open to new ideas and new techniques. They *felt* the need to improve. Outside of the seminar, the principals had been reading materials that outlined effective communication strategies. Although they generally agreed with these ideas, they hadn't really experienced a need for them until they realized that their normal approach wasn't working the way they wanted. At this point, we did the role play again. This time, I played the role of the principal (at their request), using the new techniques, while the principals played the teacher roles. Through this activity, they experienced the impact of alternative strategies and this tangible evidence served as an incentive to experiment, to try different approaches.

Some of the new techniques came from class readings. The I-message, described in Chapter 3, is a highly effective descriptive feedback technique widely described in the literature on interpersonal communication. Following a classroom presentation, which included practice sessions and demonstrations (like the role play described above), the principals were asked to use the I-message three to four times during the following week—in their homes, in phone conversations, in their work contacts. Through these experiences, they were able to test the new techniques. Even though the theory behind these messages is easily accepted, it is only when the person experiences the power of the technique that there's an incentive to use it. In addition, as the following example shows, as they reflected on their own efforts, they developed an even greater awareness of their behavior.

After their experiments with the I-message, John reported that, when he was able to use that form, he had found it very effective; but he also reported that he had a lot of difficulty using it because sometimes he delayed communicating his concerns until his frustration level was so great that he lost control of the situation and lashed out.

Abby said she had the opposite problem: that she wanted to strike out right away and had to hold back. Building on these experiences, we analyzed the problem. John concluded that he should try to address problems when he first notices them. Abby talked about ways that she tried to deal with her own weakness. She said that now she'll walk out of a trying situation rather than risk blowing up although she knows that it is only a temporary solution.

The principals also developed ideas for new strategies from their field observations and experiences. While they were in the schools, I asked them to observe their principal partners, focusing specifically on those aspects of practice that they wanted to improve. Abby, for example, wanted to learn how to create a cooperative school climate. Sara wanted to learn to empower teachers. John wanted to become a more effective supervisor and be better able to plan, delegate, and communicate. Toward those objectives, they watched and tried to identify effective strategies used by their colleagues. In working with their principal partners, they saw others struggling with similar perplexing problems and discovered approaches that had not occurred to them before. As one indicated, it was a time to "see a variety of different organizational styles that I really was unaware of" and "to look at innovations—how you divide a school up into small components, how you *really* empower teachers, how you can arrange the schedule to allow for staff development."

Through these activities, the principals became aware of problems in their administrative practice and developed a new understanding of their behavior and the thinking that shaped their behavior (theories-in-use). Once this awareness had been aroused, they began to consider new ideas and to experiment with new behaviors. At this point, the seminar shifted from a retrospective to a prospective view. The final objective of the seminar was to enable the principals not only to develop new ideas and skills but to have the opportunity to become comfortable enough with them so that they would become an integral part of their behavior. While the previous activities had examined prior experience, now the activities looked forward: What will you do when you return to the principalship? Several tasks addressed that objective. The first, a variation of the administrative platform, was to develop their vision, to outline as concretely as possible a written statement of what they wanted to accomplish and the strategies necessary to realize that vision. In a later activity, the principals developed and reviewed their plans for reentry: When they had their assignments, what would they do initially? Finally, they prepared an initial address to the faculty in their schools and presented it to our group.

These activities provided an opportunity to test and further refine their theories and experiment with new ideas and techniques. When we were reviewing administrative platform statements, it was possible to detect continued inconsistencies between intent and action. In outlining her plan for staff development, for example, Abby had made no provision to incorporate teachers' views. As a follow-up, I asked her to interview three teachers about their views on staff development. She returned from these interviews with a new respect for teacher knowledge and commitment. The assignment, which she originally dismissed as a useless activity, led her to revise her views on teachers and staff development. The interviews also gave her an opportunity to try one of the new communication skills that we had been working on: listening. Not only was she amazed at what the teachers said, she was also surprised at how favorably the teachers had received her. Despite her initial resistance to the task, she was concerned enough to give it a try; when she did, the positive response helped reinforce her efforts to change her behavior.

Developing the reentry plan provided more information. While they all defined the task as learning about the school and beginning to establish a support network, each approached the situation in a slightly different way. Sara apparently had been giving this a great deal of thought (which she confirmed) and outlined a detailed and comprehensive plan that very clearly reflected her intention to work in a cooperative manner with district and school personnel as well as community. Her plan called for initial meetings with the district superintendent to obtain information and to clarify communication followed by a general meeting with the entire staff as well as additional meetings with various constituencies. John's plan, in comparison, reflected a predominantly political orientation and called for meeting with custodians, police, local politicians, and union representatives within the building and district. There was no mention of meeting with teachers.

Changes

All of the activities in the seminar—case records, role plays, platform statements, plans, and simulations—as concrete examples of behavior, clearly reflected theories-in-use and helped to identify problem areas. By the end of the semester, through this continuous and cyclical process of experience, observation and analysis, reconceptualization, and experimentation, it was quite apparent—to the principals themselves, to the PDC staff members, the field partners, and former colleagues—that changes were taking place. All of them developed a greater level of self-awareness and self-confidence, learning to acknowledge their weaknesses and to appreciate their strengths. Sara, for example, spoke of initial doubts about her own leadership and her new appreciation of her ability: "I'm not perfect; but I am confident, and I have some skills. What matters is to be aware of what you do. Sometimes you do things out of rote without really thinking of how it is related to a total picture—I don't think I'll ever do that again." Abby described her growing awareness that she had neglected important dimensions of school leadership:

> I focused on certain areas so that I would be insulated from criticism. I didn't focus on interpersonal skills. . . . I didn't maximize the potential that the school had. . . . I said this is the plan, you will do this, you will follow this, and I didn't realize how many people I would alienate and how much more progress I could make by just changing the way I saw things.

They all developed a clearer sense of purpose as illustrated in John's comment:

> Just being away from the building—away from all of the problems and pressures, gave me a chance to reflect, to step aside and look at the way I do things and why, and where I wanted to go and how I was going to do it—like planning for battle. I was in the battle and I spent so much time putting out the fires that I never really thought about where we were going. Now I have a clearer vision of where I want to go and what I would like to do.

They all left the program with new communication skills and with techniques to resolve conflicts, solve problems, and run better meetings. They became more adept at listening and learned to "brake" their impatience. Their thinking became more clear and focused, more on target. As they clarified their thinking, their writing skills improved as well.

The most obvious changes were in their attitudes and behaviors toward each other. Initially, the principals were wary of one another and overtly critical. John recalled, for example, how he had been attacked by Abby because he had forgotten his glasses. "What kind of a principal are you?" she said. "You come to this meeting and you don't even have your glasses with you." She then told him in no uncertain terms that he was incompetent. He decided to ignore her. Sara had her mind set to disregard both of the others even before they met. At the first meeting, her decision became even firmer. Recollecting that occasion at a later date, she confided:

> You [Abby] came in like a kid who comes in tough to school, and I was going to show you that I was just as tough as you were so I wasn't going to deal with you. When he [John] came in I was very angry with him because I felt that he let them [the central office] get him and there was no reason. I was really mad at him because I felt the system had crushed him, and he shouldn't have let it happen.

Eventually, the mutual criticisms and antagonisms among them gave way; by the time the program was finished, the three principals were part of a caring and supportive team. Although they brought different personalities, strengths, and weaknesses, they learned from one another and developed a deep mutual respect and liking. As John commented about his aggressive colleague:

> I learned later on that she has a lot of good ideas, and seeing the change in the way she functioned then and the way she functions now, I picked up that sometimes you have to be a little pushy . . . not as pushy as *she* was, but sometimes you have to be a little pushy and tell people "look, this is where I'm coming from and this is what I want done."

They were also beginning to interact with others in a very different way. Abby, for example, recounted the following incident that had taken place during her field placement. An auditor from the state was visiting the school, and the principal asked her to stay with the state representative during the day to answer questions and to resolve problems. The auditor tried to discourage Abby from remaining with her but Abby persisted and said that that was the way it was going to be. She had been told to stay with her and, if a problem came up, she wanted to take care of it before the report was written. Then, she reconsidered her behavior and tried a more understanding approach using the I-message, explaining that she was there to help, not to make trouble, and that she wanted to work with the person. They finished the day; and, before leaving, the auditor confessed that she hadn't wanted Abby to stay with her because of all the terrible things she had heard about Abby. The auditor wanted Abby to know that she was not at all like what had been said and that she would be sure to tell people at the State Education Department.

In the reflective practice context with its emphasis on effective communication, particularly active listening and descriptive feedback, the principals became less defensive, more open to others' views, more empathic, and more open to the possibilities of collaborative leadership. Through their interaction with one another, they came to the same conclusion as the teachers in the TDOC project (Berkey et al., 1990): They were not only interested in others' views but also better able to accept differences of opinion and to see things from the others' perspectives. Sara talked about an incident with John that would have made her angry in the past but no longer had the same effect: "He was expressing his feelings and his feelings have to do with him. My feelings have to do with me so I don't feel as threatened now by other people's feelings as I may have in the past." Each of them had come into the program with a clear idea of what was valuable and not valuable, but they left with a realization that, if teachers and administrators don't talk about what they value and come to consensus, they as principals won't be able to make any substantive changes. All of them described a new sense of empathy for teachers' lack of independence and a heightened awareness of teachers as "growing professionals."

The Change Process

These changes, however, did not come about in a smooth or predictable manner. Following a presentation on reflective practice to a group of faculty, one of my university colleagues remarked that I made it sound so easy. Although I do think that reflective practice is a powerful process that can lead to change in a way that few other processes can, it is neither simple nor easy. Nor is it always successful. In this situation, the intensity of the observed changes may have been largely attributable to several factors, including the personal characteristics of these principals. They were caring, intelligent, well educated (one held a doctorate in educational administration), and intensely committed to improving the quality of education for urban students, particularly minority students. Like their colleagues everywhere, there were areas of their performance that could be improved; unlike many of their colleagues, each of them had been caught in volatile political situations. They were also unusually open about their own flaws and failures and anxious to become more effective. The nature of the program itself was also somewhat unusual in its size, scope, intensity, and level of support: The reflective practice seminar was not an isolated learning situation but, as Sara describes later, one strand in a tapestry of tightly woven experiences. Even under the best of circumstances, however, change is difficult and demanding, as the following example illustrates.

During the program, Abby began to speak of herself as "the old Abby" and "the new Abby" to describe her struggle to change. While new ideas easily replaced the old, it was difficult to replace old ways of acting with the new; tenacious habits of behavior would not easily be displaced even when the previous actions clearly were ineffective. Realizing now the negative effects of her domineering behavior, she went through several weeks of silence when she refused to participate in discussions at all rather than risk the reemergence of "old" behaviors. During the subsequent weeks, she participated in a very self-conscious and self-limiting way. It was not until the final session of the program that a new voice—integrating the best of the new and the old—emerged. In this session, she presented a speech prepared for her initial meeting with her old school staff. For me, this presentation clearly illustrated the changes in this person and the difficulty of the change process.

Most striking were changes in her appearance and demeanor. When the program began, her body language clearly conveyed distrust and unwillingness to engage in the process or with others in any personal way. Her eyes were withdrawn and distant, and she was tense, restless, and likely to walk out when the discussion turned to someone other than herself. In this last session, as in the previous two sessions, the "new" principal was in evidence: a warm, open, smiling, effusive, and embracing person who demonstrated through her language and manner a sensitivity, empathy, and deep understanding of herself and of others; a person who was no less committed, no less cognizant of the political, economic, and social realities shaping schools, but a person whose repertoire and choice of means were dramatically different.

Although there was no question that she had changed, it was also clear to all of us—and particularly to Abby herself—that the process was only beginning. Over the course of the program, she had come to appreciate both the difficulty of acting in accordance with her best intentions and the difficulty of behavioral change. Most people find it difficult to "practice what they preach." For this principal, this task was even more difficult: Her ideas about organizational behavior and processes had changed dramatically, but she had not yet had the experience of enacting these new beliefs in the administrative role. While she had begun to develop a new philosophy, she still needed to unlearn old behaviors at the same time that she was trying to develop new ones.

At the completion of the program, she would return to the same school she had left, and this prospect was troubling. She recognized that "the old principal" was an autocrat who dominated staff and achieved her goals by sheer force and determination, "by whatever means necessary." She also recognized that she had chosen staff who shared that approach and had a vested interest in seeing her maintain the status quo. She feared that when she returned to the school she might fall—or get pushed—into old patterns of behavior and be unable to act in accordance with the new philosophy she was developing. This was a realistic concern. So, in her presentation, she wanted to convince her audience that she was returning as a "new principal." She wanted to explain who this new person was and the meaning of her personal change for the school.

She began by emphasizing that "my mission hasn't changed, but my ideology has, my platform has." Describing the effect of those changes, she continued:

> You will never hear me say again "by any means necessary." I have become a better human being. No one who would work with me would say I've not been changed. I can listen now. I'm more sensitive. I want to help now; but I want to help in a different way. I want to be a member, not the leader, not the mama. Watch me! Let's see if what I say and my actions are the same. I'm still strong but in a real sense: it's not *my* strength but the *family's* strength.

This metaphor of the family shaped much of her presentation and she used this means to contrast her former behavior with her vision for the future. Using the words of Dr. Martin Luther King, Jr., she asked for the support and understanding of the staff: "I may not be all that I can be; I am not all that I will be, but thank God, I ain't what I was. Give me a chance," she said, "give me what I didn't give you."

In terms of her mission, she talked about the need to restructure the school to better meet the needs of kids, and she proposed establishing minischools within the large school, a proposal that she wanted to be shaped by the teachers. She emphasized the importance of student motivation and self-realization and the need for the entire "family" to work together for the kids. While particularly sensitive to the needs of the minority community, her perspective was far broader, and her standards of equity and concern for children crossed racial and ethnic lines.

Her presentation can only be described as charismatic. At the beginning of this program, her oratorical skills were quite evident. What was very evident in this presentation was that these powerful oratorical skills were now being used to convey a different message, not a message of power, control, and coercion but a message of caring, unity, and direction.

Even Abby's experience may not adequately reflect the anguish, anxiety, and uncertainty that the participants and I, as facilitator, experienced in this process. In retrospect, it is easy to remember the good times. At its conclusion, this program was viewed as a success by everyone who participated: the principals, the facilitators, the program coordinator, the mentors, and the field supervisors. But, during the project, there was no certainty that this happy conclusion was at the end of the road—far to the contrary. Many times, particularly after a grueling session, optimism was a scarce resource. The beliefs outlined in the reflective practice credo were sorely tested.

One of the assumptions that people often make about reflective practice has to do with participants' receptivity: "Well, it may work if people are open to it." But this situation challenged that assumption. None of the principals was totally enthusiastic on entering the program; Abby, in particular, made it quite clear through her comments and her actions that she was angry and resentful of the process that she viewed as a waste of time. "I wasn't too pleased . . . I was making it up in my mind to exclude this part from it because I really didn't see where you could be of very much help. I thought I knew administrative leadership. I had gone through a doctoral program in administration. There's nothing you can add." Although the other principals were not as openly antagonistic, they were angry and somewhat bitter at having been put into the program. It took time for them to begin to think positively and look on the project as anything other than a punishment.

The participants entered the program with strong feelings, and the process itself generates strong feelings and occasionally anger. Developing a conscious awareness of your own performance is critical for reflection, but this process of coming face-to-face with certain aspects of your own performance can be threatening and often provokes strong feelings, even under the best of conditions. I would venture to say that the emotional intensity is greater where the greatest learning is taking place. The very thing that makes reflective practice so powerful—the personalization of the process, or confronting one's own beliefs and actions—is also the aspect that makes it difficult. As Abby explained, she was comfortable as long as I talked about theory, but, when I left that domain, "that's when I got dissatisfied.

When you left the theory and started coming with the role playing and integrating all of it, that's when I became unhappy." This unhappiness was expressed in the classroom in a variety of distressing behaviors. During one session, for example, Abby reported on a workshop experience, but, for the rest of the time, she was uninvolved in the task, refused to provide feedback to either John or Sara, fiddled with papers while others were talking, and walked out early. The next week, she said that she had done it intentionally: that she wanted to get back at me (about feedback that I had given her) and knew that was the way to do it. This was one of the first times that she had been willing to be so open about her feelings. Even though I knew at the time that these experiences are to be expected as the participants react to feedback, it was difficult not to take the reactions personally, and sessions like these were emotionally draining.

Despite the discomfort—theirs and mine—it was this personalization, being forced to go beyond theory and to look at themselves in action, that made the impact. As Sara explained:

> This was professional growth that was tied in to who I was as a person. In the past, it was just the acquisition of skills: I learned by going to conferences but it didn't involve a key examination of who I was as a human being. This program required me to look at myself as a person and as a professional—to self-evaluate; to see why I am the way I am, why certain things bother me; to put things into perspective.

Assessing the Program

The learning process in the seminar was enriched by the wide array of learning opportunities provided in the other three strands of the Professional Development Center program. In a sense, the principals' experience was like a hall of mirrors. All of their activities—describing critical incidents and reenacting problem situations; developing mission statements and action plans; visiting schools and observing principals and teachers working together in different ways; working with mentors, facilitators, and counselors; completing

personality inventories as part of business-sponsored workshops—
provided information that helped the principals to see themselves in
different ways and to envision new possibilities. In role plays, they
saw how their words, actions, and mannerisms affected others. Looking at the results of a leadership style inventory, they discovered that,
in some cases, they were "using the wrong style for the wrong situation or doing things by rote without really thinking how it relates
to a total picture." Writing a vision statement and designing an action
plan "made me really think about what I believed and realize that,
while I may have succeeded in some ways, I didn't maximize the
potential that the school had." As Sara explained, being in the
program was like being at the center of a circle with many threads:

> All the threads came together amazingly well, but I'm the one
> who had to take all these strings and weave them together. As
> we were talking about collaborating with staff or running a
> meeting that would get people to talk, at the same time, I was
> looking at myself as a leader and watching others as leaders;
> and I began to tie it together.

While the experiences were themselves informative and enlightening, the opportunity to obtain direct feedback of a kind they did
not normally receive from supervisors, staff, and colleagues also
contributed to their growing self-awareness. In the reflective practice seminar as well as in other strands of the project, the program
staff emphasized and modeled honest and open communication. The
purpose of the program was to enable these principals to be more
effective. To become more effective, they had to have clear ideas of
where the problems were: an awareness of what they had being doing
that did not work. Designing their own agendas, analyzing case
studies, reenacting and reevaluating troubling experiences from the
past, outlining their vision statements and action plans for the future,
observing and talking with their principal partners, mentors, and
teachers—all provided the opportunity to identify problems and
obtain feedback about their performance. They were told when they
made others feel angry, hurt, or defensive. They were told when their
ideas were unclear or when their actions seemed inconsistent with

their beliefs and goals. Provided with feedback, being able to see their reflection through the eyes of their colleagues, they began to see the discrepancies between their espoused beliefs and their actions, between their intentions and their accomplishments. As Sara commented, "Being able to see the inconsistencies gave me more thought for reflection." It was a critical process, but it was also supportive. Provided with encouragement and alternative strategies, the principals were then able to experiment with new ideas and strategies in a critical but caring environment.

The variety of experiences, access to descriptive feedback and opportunities for reflection, and behavioral experimentation contributed to the development of new perspectives. Reflective practice, because of its specific emphasis on personal development and responsibility, also affected the outcomes. As the principals explained, the approach to leadership they encountered was unlike any prior experience:

> This program focused on interpersonal skills—not skills of control. It was looking at leadership from the perspective of the people who have to work with you. In the 70's there wasn't much emphasis on human aspects of organizations. I was trained to beat the system, how to beat the teachers, how to beat the superintendent. There wasn't enough emphasis on competence—in the things that matter for kids. I'm not anti-intellectual, but I think that everything has to be put into the context of human relations that make an organization work. People make organizations work and we have to learn how to work with people.

Because of this human resource emphasis that is integral to reflective practice, the principals were very attuned to personal needs and feelings and came to understand how their own feelings affect their performance and how their actions affect others, particularly teachers and students. With new understanding of their actions and effects, old theories-in-use gave way to new ones. The realization that sheer force, determination, and control do not create harmony and love for learning, for example, led Sara to a belief that "teacher empowerment is important to help me achieve what I want to achieve for kids, and the only way I can empower people is through collaboration and involving them in the things they're going to be responsible for."

RETURNING TO THE PRINCIPALSHIP

At the end of the semester, as I mentioned, changes were evident, but a major question remained: What would happen when they returned to their schools?

In January 1992, Abby returned to her former school and found, as she had anticipated, her former allies tightly aligned against her and her efforts to change. Her reputation and her previous actions were a legacy that now worked against her. Despite the obstacles, however, she steadfastly held to her new vision and continued to work with her superiors, colleagues, and advisers in her effort to resolve the administrative problems she faced. In the past, Abby had been singled out by the United Federation of Teachers (UFT) because of her dealings with teachers: On taking over one school, for example, she was responsible for forcing the departure of nearly the entire teaching staff. In the year she returned, she was cited publicly by the union for introducing a team governance structure for the school through which she as principal shares decision-making authority with administrators, teachers, parents, and district representatives.

Sara and John entered new schools and literally had the opportunity to start fresh. At the end of the year, I scheduled a visit with John to talk about the principalship: Was he any different as a principal now than he had been when he first entered the PDC? We met in his office and, during the course of the following hour, I not only had the chance to listen to him but to watch him as he interacted with teachers, administrators, and students. What I saw were some obvious—and, to me, amazing—differences between the principal who walked into the first session and the principal I was watching.

When John began the PDC, he described himself as a principal who bore the responsibility for the entire school on his own shoulders. He had difficulty delegating because he didn't trust others to do the work well, and he was extremely reluctant to confront staff members about problems. As he explained later, he lacked a clear-cut vision or goals, demonstrated little evidence of strategic planning, and relied on his formal authority as the principal to exercise control. In general, he appeared to be harried, frustrated, and prone to losing his temper.

During the course of the interview, it became apparent that these characteristics no longer applied. At a personal level, he described himself as relaxed, more comfortable, more in control, and less stressed. Now, he says, he interacts with his teachers in a very different way:

> I do more talking and more counseling and more understanding than I did before. I'm trying to deal with students and staff not as a "principal" but as someone who has problems and who may understand and be able to help with their problems. I can call people to the office, and they don't come in worried about what they've done. There are no threats, no yelling, no screaming.

Where before he relied on his position as principal, he turns instead to information: "Before I controlled with the title. Now I throw the title out the window explaining the reason why and getting people to buy into it. I provide a lot of information so that people will understand why they're being asked to do things."

He explained that recently, for example, he had met with all of the teachers to explain the allotment system for teaching positions, as part of his yearlong effort to increase attendance at the school. He also described himself as being more reflective:

> I think a lot more. I ponder things. I do more planning. I have time to think about what I've done and how I've reacted: Was there another way? I think about the things that I didn't have time to do or that I need to do: to meet with someone because I was too brusque. I spend a lot more time in self-evaluation. Before I was so busy defending myself or running around that I didn't have time to develop new strategies. I feel better about what I'm trying to do because I see the little successes. I realize what I'm doing.

In contrast with his previous approach, which he described as "putting out fires," he spends more time in planning and concentrates his attention on clearly defined goals; the vision is clear and the plan is comprehensive. In terms of boosting attendance, for example:

> There are a million things that need to be done. Teachers have to buy into the procedures; they have to be willing to fill out the forms and make the follow-up phone calls. The form letters to parents needed to be prepared and the disciplinary procedures needed to be outlined. We had to redo the back office procedures to make sure that we had daily attendance records; we had to get the people in the back office to work toward a common goal.

His managerial strategies also reflect a different philosophical approach. In describing how he worked with the staff to raise attendance in the school, it was clear that he had adopted a number of strategies common to transformational leaders: He had created a vision and used that vision to engage teachers and staff in the change process. As part of his efforts to improve school attendance, he met with the entire staff and explained his goal—to improve attendance —and his rationale—to serve kids, and to ask their assistance: "I'm the principal but this isn't a one-man show. I'm the one who's ultimately responsible but you're vital to me. I need you to do the job. We work as a team here; I need your help."

During the interview, it was apparent that John spent a lot of time talking to teachers about problems—and that he was quite comfortable. As part of his plan to increase attendance, he kept daily records of family group attendance and provided the information to all the teachers. When attendance was low, he contacted the teachers to inform them and ask them to continue their efforts. Charts showing attendance data for the last 2 years were on the wall, and I watched as he met with a teacher about a related problem. During these conversations, he seemed comfortable, relaxed, and at ease. Although he had had relatively little time to develop skill in using the I-message format during the seminar, it was evident in his language now. "Listen," he began, "I have a problem . . . we have a problem. You've put me in an uncomfortable position." He then proceeded to explain what happened and why he was concerned: the teacher had sent a new student out of her classroom because of overcrowding and the student left the building.

I reminded him of his comments during the seminar about his reluctance to deal with problems. Now, he responded, he had found a way to get things done without confrontation. Before, if there was paper on the floor, he would have told someone to pick it up and expected them to do it because he (the principal) said to pick it up. Now, he would deal with it differently: I know you didn't put it there, but we're trying to create a certain atmosphere here. We have to keep focusing on goals.

Sara, like John, recognized differences in her new principalship. Like John, she reported that she thinks more, makes fewer unilateral decisions, and spends a great deal more time and effort talking with teachers and trying to involve them more in decision making. When she talks, she's more likely to say "we" than "I" and realizes that she can't rely on the power of the principalship to get things done. She also sees herself as more mellow, less likely to get upset in the face of disagreement or resistance, and more attuned to teacher needs than in the past: "Before, I was much more kid-oriented. Not that I was ever anti-teacher, but now I try to balance the kid-orientation with a teacher-orientation. Now teachers say 'we know you're pro-kid, Sara.' They also know that I'm pro-teacher."

Reflecting on the changes, Sara commented that she didn't know how much is her own personal growth and how much is the situation. The environment is one of trust: "There's a nice camaraderie." The school itself is much smaller, which "makes it easier to personalize and to see others as individuals: there's less of a necessity to get people to march to the same drum." She also describes the staff and supervisors in positive terms: The teachers are more open, less likely to say "no," and more committed to the kids. The supervisors, too, are "good people to work with: They help you carry your agenda." Although she feels that her core has never changed, she's still working to resolve problems. She comments: "I have more acceptance that there are challenges we have to overcome together. . . . I've reconceptualized power: It's solidified in my head that you can't have it unless others let you have it."

Her commitment to shared decision making prompted her efforts to develop a constitution to formalize the working but loose structure operating in the school. While this year's teacher representatives are all volunteers, next year, she hopes to enfranchise more of the staff through elections and to incorporate students in a meaningful way. While she's eager to move ahead with curricular reform—this year, "we" implemented a dropout prevention demonstration project in collaboration with a nearby college and introduced a house structure to respond to the personal and academic needs of ninth and tenth graders—she recognizes that "you can't mandate a curriculum."

In Chapter 1, we discussed the role of reflective practice in creating personal and organizational change. In this situation, each principal returned to work with renewed enthusiasm, a new vision, and an expanded repertoire of leadership strategies. While it would be unreasonable to expect that they would be able to transform difficult urban schools in demanding organizational environments, they have made progress in creating schools that are more humane and more responsive to the needs of staff and students. Nonetheless, this path to change was neither smooth nor straight. In reentering the system, each encountered difficulties, made mistakes, and experienced discouragement; but, when confronted with problems, support was available.

Although the formal portion of the renewal program was complete, the principals still remained part of a learning community. When they encountered difficulties and made mistakes, as part of the ongoing support provided by Bank Street Professional Development Center, they were able to discuss their problems with advisers, consider new alternatives, change direction, and try again. The principals had access to external and nonjudgmental support, and they were willing and able to identify their problems and seek out advice. The principals were also fortunate to have supportive supervisors in their own districts who further facilitated their efforts to change. This support from colleagues and from organizational superiors is no doubt important in determining the probability of successful change.

In concluding, reflective practice seems to stimulate a change process that, once begun, doesn't end. By helping people to develop skills of critical analysis that they can apply to their own practice, it changes professional practice from an impersonal process that takes place during a restricted period of time in a classroom to an ongoing process that becomes integrated into one's professional life. It does not claim to eliminate problems of practice but to establish a process for examining and responding to those problems in new and more varied ways.

NOTE

1. Sections of this chapter are drawn from a previous paper (Osterman & Sullivan, 1992).

7

School Leaders Engaging in Reflection: A Stimulus to Systemic Change

QUESTIONS AND A SERENDIPITOUS OPPORTUNITY

Success, as well as failure, may lead to reflection. After years of successful teaching and student self-reported learning with "The Reflective Administrator" course described in Chapter 5, I began to ask questions. Over time, the concept of culture had become a powerful element in my thinking about organizations. And some students had told me that, while the course helped them to change themselves on a personal level, they were having difficulty influencing their organizations, especially some superiors, to support and spread a reflective posture. I began to ask whether my work with *individuals* drawn out of their normal work and cultural contexts in the course might not be parallel to what was learned about individual participation in T-groups in the 1960s.

While this human potential movement had profound individual effects, many found insights developed in the isolation of the group experience difficult to use upon returning to their families and work settings. Families and workplaces have cohesive cultures, including sets of norms and behavioral expectations. Individuals returning from

T-groups to these cultures found strong social forces arrayed to keep them conforming to their "old" behaviors and few forces to support experimentation with their "new" behaviors. While T-group participants reported powerful individual effects on themselves, effects on their organizations were more difficult to find. Might it not be the same with reflection?

I focused on several questions: What would happen if I could facilitate reflection in an intact work group? Would individual positive effects of reflection be multiplied by developing a supportive workplace culture? Could a group reflection arrangement become a powerful engine for organizational improvement? Was it possible to facilitate reflective practice in a hierarchical group where authentic participation had direct career implications?

With these questions posed, I attended a conference in which a local superintendent designate made a presentation called "Synergetic Supervision." Serendipity occurred. I heard in his presentation assumptions similar to those underlying reflective practice and my attempts to facilitate it: clear intentions, descriptively delivered performance feedback, mutual trust, the centrality of effective communication. We talked. We clearly shared important values and assumptions. He had a districtwide context in which to attempt work group reflection. I had a conceptual framework and experience that made sense to him.

Several weeks later, I was invited, along with curriculum theorist colleague Janet Miller, to a meeting in his district to explore possibilities for an administrator-professor reflection group. Not knowing what to expect, Janet and I accepted. Arrayed at the meeting were all of the district administrators. The exchange was strange. No women spoke. Men principals spoke in rank order. Critical questions were couched in religious metaphors, and it was charged that reflection was a means of indoctrination. (We learned later that some members of the principals' union were carrying out a job action as part of a salary dispute at this time.) Janet and I left the meeting quite puzzled and with no clear notion of what would come of it.

Several weeks later, we were invited to meet with the administrators who had chosen to engage with us. Following the meeting, the superintendent had sent a memo to all administrators. He intended to work on reflection with us; others who wished to join were welcome. When we assembled during September, members included the superintendent, the director of curriculum and student personnel services, director of language arts and testing, two elementary principals, and two Hofstra professors. The newly appointed associate superintendent joined us at the second or third meeting. The group contained four men and four women.

UNCHARTED WATERS AND THE EVOLVING MYSTERY

At the first meeting, we sought to get our bearings. None of us knew exactly what it meant to develop this kind of reflection group. The school district members likely thought that Janet and I knew what to do, but we were not certain about direction. We each had conducted reflective experiences from clear leadership positions. But this was new ground. I consciously entered this situation as an experiment and desired to play two different roles: group member and observer-researcher. To be an authentic participant meant to seek a role other than professor, one in charge, or one supposed to have answers. In fact, Janet and I were not hired to be consultants or experts. But to be a group member did not mean that I put into abeyance my considerable knowledge and experience in facilitating reflection and group communication processes. All of us, however, were engaged in finding roles for ourselves as the group experience unfolded. It was something new for each of us.

I recall a quite open first discussion about the great uncertainty involved in this venture. We came to consensus on several things. First, although we were not clear where this venture would lead, everyone was willing to begin the voyage. Second, we agreed to meet during regular work time, making group experience part of regular work for us all. Third, we decided to begin working together by exploring some of the means Janet and I had developed in the past. She described the use of personal narratives (Miller, 1988, 1990b), and I noted the writing and testing of educational and administrative platforms (Kottkamp, 1982, 1990b). We left, all agreeing to write a narrative for sharing at the next meeting. The topic, suggested by Janet, was a vivid memory of power and authority from our experiences as students.

All took this task seriously and shared narratives at the second meeting. The recollections were carefully crafted, many of a literary character. They included detailed descriptions of settings, persons, actions, and reactions and brought up vivid images employing multiple senses. They explored deep emotions as well as external events. One person described the shock of her teacher giving away the secret of Santa Claus when she still "believed." One person detailed being held on the ground and told to kiss the shoe of a cleric as punishment for defying his authority on the playground. Janet attended a parochial school in second grade. But, because she was not Roman Catholic, she was excluded from catechism class. This was accomplished, however, by placing her in the hallway without explanation. Convinced she had been "bad," she was fearful as she sought in vain to discover what she had done wrong. I recounted the powerful mixed message in a comment affixed below the letter "A" on a three-page college paper I had spent most of a Christmas holiday writing: "A rather amazing performance, if this is your work."

Sharing personal narratives was an important way for us to begin our corporate venture. It was not "business as usual," as we came to say. We presented our whole selves, emotional as well as intellectual —something we don't usually do in formal work meetings. It reduced the differences in our positions and authority bases. It helped us to be genuine and, as we later saw it, to begin the process of building a special kind of trust in each other. It also gave us some deeply etched images—mostly negative—about the effects of schooling on students, images that became shared metaphors and touchstones to which we returned again and again in our explorations of our work and professional practices. We experienced the import of our pasts for what we do in the current time. In reflective terms, we confronted our own acculturation processes, values, and assumptions predominant in school culture and in our own theories-in-use. It was, in fact, an excellent beginning both to reflection itself and for building a group culture for reflection to flourish.

The next several meetings were general discussions. Janet and I spoke about some of the related studies, writing, and questions on which we were working. The administrators filled us in on specifics of the district. We did some reading, mostly articles Janet and I had written about reflection and associated issues (Kottkamp, 1982, 1990a; Miller, 1988, 1990b). I later learned that several members perceived this as "professors assigning homework" and declined to do it. Janet and I were knowledgeable "authorities" in something the others knew little about, so no doubt we were acting in more of an authority role than I would now espouse; certainly we were perceived that way. Janet and I did use our expertise but did not, in my view, dominate the group. This early period was a time for testing out others and the group, testing for a sense of trust, position, and evolving norms.

Three noteworthy events—two of them later recounted in individual interviews I conducted with each administrator about a year and a half after the group started—occurred during these early meetings. Each was critical for developing trust and openness among the group members. First, the superintendent deliberately moved from sitting at the head of the long table to the side. All others saw and "read" the symbol he was creating about his position in the group, moving from the acknowledged power seat to an undifferentiated position. It was a clear signal about a new role—group member—that he was taking on in this setting. Since then, only on rare occasions has anyone sat at either end of the table.

The second event was the presentation of two platforms. I suggested writing platforms as we had written narratives. I gave a short introduction to platforms and included my platform for "The Reflective Administrator" course (reproduced in Figure 5.1 in Chapter 5). The director of language arts and testing made an oral presentation toward the end of a session. I recall a positive response but also remember wishing I had had a written copy to ponder and wishing there had been more time to discuss his beliefs. The superintendent volunteered second. He seemed quite eager, and the group actually put him off for two sessions, largely because of other matters being discussed and in the second instance because of a recognized lack of time at the end of a session. That he presented his platform, and in written form with copies for all, was another critical incident, a

Figure 7.1. The Superintendent's Platform

I feel that flexibility and a tolerance for ambiguity are essential attributes that I need to cultivate to lead a school district's staff. To further develop these attributes and to become more effective as a superintendent, I avoid asking questions that begin with "why," and I try to think in the following terms:

> How do things occur the way they do?
> How can we improve?
> What can we do?
> Who can do it best?

A sense of collegiality, of sharing ideas, values, perceptions, and feelings, is important to me. I believe that an educational institution must have many open channels of communication as well as clearly identified points of responsibility. One of my responsibilities is to model the behavior and the values that represent the ideals of the school district. For me, the primary behaviors are listening, exchanging ideas, analyzing, and evaluating outcomes.

A personal orientation toward action and results seems important if the school district is to be energized for growth and improvement. Also, all people should feel important and valued. I feel I must take time to get to know all our employees better and to appreciate their contributions to our services better.

second major symbol. He was metaphorically "laying himself on the table" for the rest of us to scrutinize (see Figure 7.1 for the actual platform). It sent a message that he trusted us, that he wanted to get feedback on where he stood, that he was open to learning. We all interpreted it as a statement about power, control, trust, and willingness to engage in authentic learning about self. Trust and willingness for others to put themselves "on the table" grew tremendously with this symbolic action. The discussion of the platform was short, and it was never raised again. It is the shortest platform I have ever seen, yet it is a concise and useful statement of espoused theory in the sense that descriptive performance feedback on his intended outcomes could easily be given to him. Later in the chapter, I will present some evidence concerning his behavior and its relationship to his platform.

The third event occurred in the third session when Janet and I asked permission to tape-record the meetings. In the first meeting, we had described our intention of studying the experiment we were also part of and had discussed a bit about using naturalistic or qualitative methods of data collection. In asking permission to record, we stipulated that at any point any member had the right to request no taping. The tape has run at every meeting and has never been turned off. Permission giving was a third clear symbol of evolving trust. By now, I doubt that participants are even consciously aware of the tape recorder sitting in the middle of the table at each session.

Transition occurred again at the fifth session. Janet and I said very little until the very end. We were clearly not in charge, and we were not doing any of "our things." Rather, the conversation was a serial progression of issues and problems the district and these administrators were confronting. It was not a deeply reflective discussion. At one level, it filled Janet and me in on information about the district that we simply lacked. At another level, it was the group members beginning to take charge for themselves. One director later characterized this meeting as achieving a level of "shoptalk," one containing no particular depth or confidences, yet a necessary prelude to conversations that did.

I consciously held myself back during this meeting and then deliberately played the role of process observer and interpreter at its end. This was, of course, playing a facilitator role. Janet also had been quiet and seemed to play a similar role in the end. We noted that a transition had occurred, that we had been largely silent, that the district members had directed and carried the discussion. I left excited, sensing that we had turned a corner and that the group would rapidly develop a functional direction—but one Janet and I could not define and would not lead.

My hunch was correct. What evolved and continues to this day, what the group invented, was a "new way of doing business," a set of norms governing group meetings that are unlike those in any other group I have experienced. My own metaphors during this evolution were "mystery" and "running on autopilot." It was as if there was something "bigger" going on here than is typical in organizations, something developing at an unspoken, almost spiritual level. In retrospect, the descriptors I applied at this point included *authentic engagement, strong commitment, risk taking, willingness to explore, playfulness, humor, incisive intellectual probing, openness to information, trust,* and *openness to explore emotions as well as thoughts.* Mystery and the sense of autopilot also merged in the sense that, without explicit discussion, the group always arrived at a meaningful destination. It was as if an unknown force was leading us toward improving ourselves and our organizations through unplanned and unstructured conversations. We were a group consistently moving toward functioning under Model II assumptions.

Mine are not the only metaphors. In later interviews, others gave me their personal meanings. For several principals, this is a "philosophical group," a place where meaningful personal and organizational issues are discussed openly, directly. The associate superintendent said this group is different than other work-related groups because we don't meet under pressure to decide or come to closure but simply to explore and learn. Several members developed the metaphor "agendaless group," a symbol sharing some of the meaning of my autopilot. *Agendaless* also carries connotations about power, authority, and control. The "agenda" is developed by the groups; no single person is in control. This group is "democratic" in a deep sense. Every person is assumed to have important contributions to make— speaking and listening contributions. Several members said we "take off our roles and leave them at the door." While this is not completely true (analysis of the tape recordings indicates that the superintendent, Janet, and I talk more frequently than others), everyone experiences less hierarchical role differentiation than in any other groups in which they are members and probably less than in any multirole group to which they have ever belonged.

It became clear early on that this group differs from all the other work-related groups we attend. It is a healthy group and produces healthy outcomes, healthy for individuals and healthy for both the school district and even the university. Individuals miss meetings only when there are overriding work responsibilities of great import or urgency. This group probably comes the closest to operating according to Model II assumptions of any group I know.

CONTENT AND THE ONGOING MYSTERY

Even though group process has a level of "mystery," the content of discussion is easily described. The agenda evolves in the meeting process of every meeting. But there are predictable regularities. We often begin with small talk, friends catching up on current happenings in work and private lives. One or more of these bits, typically within a short time, evolves into a focused discussion of a professional issue. Often, a single issue occupies the entire meeting. Most of us join in regardless of who raised the topic. The progression is typically an examination of a single incident coming from one individual, which leads to parallel or related personal experiences. The conversation has both cognitive and emotional dimensions and a pace and rhythm. Attention, careful listening, questioning, humor and fun, and deep engagement are obvious among all. The decibels rise, fall, and rise again. Graphic images abound as do metaphoric description and reasoning. Often, someone picks up a thread from a former meeting and weaves it into the fabric of the new discussion. Thus ideas and themes continue and evolve over time as new specifics spark different perspectives on common past experiences. Toward the end of a session, we begin to stand back further from the concreteness and to look at the discussion process itself, to look at issues writ large: Where have we been? What have we learned? What do we need to pursue further? What questions do we need to raise? Janet and I often took the lead in this summing up early on, but now more and more other group members foster this bringing together, this higher-level summation, this reflection on the process itself. Part of the mystery is the similar pattern of chat, specifics, exploration, and expansion from different personal perspectives, tying in of past experiences, and finally summation in the form of "philosophical" issue raising or painting the big picture, all in an agendaless group.

Such is the process, but, to get a better grasp of what happens, we need to look at content as well. In the transition period between Operations Desert Shield and Desert Storm, there was a very powerful, empowering discussion of war-related issues. Included was the relationship between a fourth-grade classroom and a soldier. They had been writing back and forth. The soldier had mentioned an absence of clouds in the desert. This sparked a whole science unit on weather that deeply engaged the students. The entire student body sent the soldier "clouds" they fashioned out of paper. Each cloud had a message, and they asked the soldier to share them with his company. He had gotten to know the children so well as individuals that he sent them individual holiday messages on cards. The discussion evolved into a concentration on the meaning of the relationship between the children and the soldier. Should he be invited to come to the classroom when he came home? What if he were killed after developing such a close relationship with these young people? How would the adults deal with it? How would they deal with the children?

From these concrete issues, the inquiry grew to a consideration of the symbol: yellow ribbon. Different groups in the district were debating the meaning of the symbol, whether it should be displayed in the schools, and what to do about students or adults who took an antiwar position. Really big issues came out: What is the meaning of war to young children? How do we deal with them vis-à-vis the contemporary situation? What are the power and place of symbols in the situation? How do we deal with death among young children should it occur to someone they know well? We referred to our own histories, many of us having come of age in the Vietnam war period. It was a riveting discussion, a kind too infrequently held among educational leaders. It was about real, contemporary, important issues. It was above all about education, children, and the meaning of education among contemporary events. It was a powerful discussion. I was away on a professional trip—the only meeting I have missed—but was able to listen to the tape. It affected me deeply. It had cognitive and emotional power. I thought deeply; at times, tears came as I listened. Questions came too: Why do we not hold more discussions like this one as educators? Why not in schools? Why not in universities? Why not at school board meetings? Reflections sparked by reflection!

I do not have details on what transpired after the conversation, though I could probably get them. What I know is that, although no formal policy was developed at the meeting itself, the discussion guided the district's approach to yellow ribbons, symbols, and protests. This was a deeply reflective session, a child- and education-centered session, a growth-producing and deeply professional session. In later interviews, this incident was universally mentioned as a watershed in group development and in the individual and corporate realization of the positive and powerful worth of the venture we were in together. In this session and those to follow, seeds sewn in faith yielded tangible, and valuable, results unavailable almost anywhere else. By this point in the group's evolution, we were hooked on whatever this mystery was, though we could not explain it. It was good for us. It was good for kids. It was bearing bountiful fruit.

We discussed typical educational issues as well. We talked at length about curriculum and pedagogy, about process-oriented instruction in writing and math. We had long inquiries and metaphorical discussions about the differences between elementary and secondary teachers' conceptions of instruction, children, and learning. We kept coming back to the issue of how secondary teachers could be supported in giving up some of their subject-matter-specialist and child-seen-only-as-student orientations for more of the whole child and interdisciplinary orientations of the elementary teachers.

During one session, we solved a problem on the spot. After one of our reflective inquiries about supporting teachers in taking risks and learning new teaching methods and ideologies, someone posed a concrete problem: We want to encourage the use of manipulative materials in elementary math, but there is no money in the budget to cover this, although there are considerable unspent funds in the "textbook" budgetary account. The most quiet member asked a telling question: "What if we called manipulative materials textbooks?" In this discussion, the superintendent dropped his typical group behavior and "played the role of superintendent," as one member later described it (meaning he displayed his hierarchical position and made a decision). He said: "Math manipulatives are textbooks; order them and I'll sign the requisitions." In the discussion that continued, I pursued the issue. The "textbook" budgetary category was put into educational regulations many years ago. Careful analysis of the assumptions (theory-in-use) underlying the textbook category also indicated notions of education and learning embedded in the law, regulation, and organizations that we are unaware of and seldom scrutinize: For education to occur, we need teachers, students, texts, and a blackboard. Pushed further, an embedded theory-in-use about information transfer, didactic presentation, and other assumptions detailed in Chapter 2 could be extracted. A specific problem resulted in "seeing" much larger issues as well as solving an issue in an educationally sound way.

Janet and I are also group members; we bring "our" issues too. One session dealt with our frustration over a number of problems at the university. (We have no reflection group like this for ourselves at the university.) It was therapeutic for us. We received attentive listening and were helped in reflecting about issues. On another occasion, I brought a personal issue from my role as parent of a public school child. My freshman son, who has a special education classification for math, was greatly fearful of his French teacher, was falling behind, and was repeating self-fulfilling prophesies of the order: "I'll study, but I know I'll flunk the test." (As I later came to learn, it was largely an issue of her perception of him as a "special ed kid," the likes of which she had not had to deal with until a recent state regulation change, as well as her staunch unwillingness to deviate from her five-periods- staying-together-on-the-same-lesson-plan approach to teaching.) In discussing "my problem," every educator parent came to tell a wrenching story about trying to deal with a teacher who was causing harm to his or her child. We ended the session by pushing the issue to broader levels of reflection, focusing once again—but in a new way—on one of our constantly repeated themes: power and authority. We asked: If we who are part of the system have great problems ourselves, what must it be like as an average parent to confront the system—to confront us—to have something rectified? Again, we identified a problem we all need to self-monitor in our professional work. We came to conscious awareness of something that mattered a great deal, something we had choices about if we were only conscious of it.

A final example illustrates different issues. The focal concern was changing the delivery structure for the elementary reading curriculum. It arose from a major funding crisis. New York State had a severe budget deficit. The governor and legislature made significant midyear reductions in state aid to public schools. Further, half of all state aid cuts were to come out of the two counties on Long Island. The district was facing a potential $5 million loss. Such a cut could not be met by trimming around the edges.

The superintendent wished to reduce the payroll by 12 teaching positions. He had been scrutinizing a primary readiness program instituted 25 years earlier, a program with considerable regional recognition and considered very successful by parents and teachers. It was also a solid part of the ideology and culture of the district. One of the principals had been the first teacher of this program and another had taught in it. There was personal history and commitment in the group as well.

The readiness program had been developed to benefit kindergarteners moving into first grade who were not maturationally prepared for a regular first-grade class. The idea was to provide more time, a different pace, and a true opportunity to allow readiness and success to evolve. Special efforts kept it from becoming a "dumping ground" for "problem" students; in it were kids who simply needed a different pace and environment. The program ran in self-contained first- and second-grade classes in each of the five elementary schools with a class size between half and two thirds of the regular class size. In a real financial crunch, this became an expensive program.

Apparently, the superintendent had framed the problem primarily in budgetary and class size terms. The district, however, also had been instituting a writing process and integrated language arts curriculum and was working on process math approaches. A "detracking" decision also had been made for ninth-grade math in the coming year. Many of these issues, especially how to provide support for teachers to get them to take the risk to attempt these new curricular and dialogical approaches, had been a continuous theme through the history of the group meetings.

Over a period of a month or more, there was a gradual redefinition of the issues surrounding the paced readiness classes covering all first- and second-grade subjects. The roots of this transition lay in principal meetings with the superintendent, individual perceptual change (especially on the part of several of the originators of the program), and discussions in the reflection group. A budgetary issue became a quality of education issue. Saving money and class size became secondary to improved instruction. What became understood is that, while the readiness program was a valuable innovation 25 years ago, and while it had provided students with special needs a more sound educational program in earlier days, today there are educationally more sound ways of achieving the same goals—which also happen to be cost effective. As the problem definition changed, changing the readiness program was viewed as contributing to the districtwide commitment to detracking students. (There was evidence that, although the readiness program did prove beneficial for many students, they were also "labeled" by others under the old program.)

During the period of considering the readiness curriculum, the effect of the reflection group was abundantly clear in one instance. A principal, the first teacher in the readiness program, reported a surprise phone call (described in Chapter 2) at one of our meetings. She is an externally calm person, but she was visibly upset. The call came from an old friend, retired for several years, who was angry at her for "betraying" the readiness program he too had helped to develop and nurture. She was surprised at the depth of his emotion. At the time of the call, she had already decided that the old program needed to be altered for educational reasons, a position she had reached partly through the work of the reflective practice group. Consequently, she had not defended it in an administrative meeting called to consider changing the program. The "word" that she did not defend the program had gotten out. Her friend, however, lacked understanding about why she had not vigorously defended the program. When she reported the surprise, she did not understand fully the caller's perspective. She later told me that the group had been of great assistance in her wrestling with the emotional undertow from the call, that reflective practice had helped her to separate criticism from the position she took, and that reflection had provided her with a means for figuring out why she was not upset by the elimination of the program—a position whereby she surprised herself. Thus the reflective group process provided her with resources for dealing with several deep emotional issues.

BEYOND CONTENT:
UNDERSTANDING REFLECTION IN A WORK GROUP CONTEXT

The reflective experience in this group was different than that in "The Reflective Administrator" course. The workings of "mystery" are such that it is not always clear to me, and I suppose to others, at any one point, what is occurring. In my course, I structure specific experiences and get feedback about them. When I structure at least an outline of events, I am more clear about what is happening. Thus, while I cannot claim group reflection "caused" the reading curriculum change to occur as it did, certainly the collaborative experience was integrally related to the way the district administrators reconceptualized and acted in this case and in many others.

In terms of the experiential learning cycle, the group experience and the members' ongoing interaction outside of the formal meetings meandered back and forth among the stages of the cycle: experience and reflection, analysis and problem definition, abstract reconceptualization, and experimentation. Participants brought concrete issues like the state budget cut and the surprise phone call to the group. Analysis, problem definition, and reconceptualization of the issues and responses resulted from the cycling of the discussions back and forth over a period of several months. Experiments took place as proposals were floated at both the reflection group and other district meetings. These proposals elicited feedback about the reconceptualizations. While individuals had their own flashes of insight and changes of perception outside of the group experience, the group was a vehicle for continuing inquiry and collaborative problem definition and solving. It was an important emotion sharing and communication center. Shared information was good and relatively unfiltered because of the high trust level. Thus, though it did not run in a neat, one-two-three-four, by-the-numbers, clearly obvious experiential learning cycle, certainly the elements of the cycle were occurring in patterns that lay just below our level of conscious awareness.

Once, after a long discussion of the impact of the state aid crisis, I asked bluntly: "So is this reflection experience of any particular use in coping with this situation, or is it irrelevant?" "Definitely helpful!" was the enthusiastic and unanimous response. The super-intendent recounted how the district mission statement he had been forging with the board of education was central to how they dealt with the crisis. He had reduced the mission to three core values—to a "bumper sticker": Quality, Service, and Growth. That is what he and the district are about. His reflection experience had been helpful in this formulation. It was this mission statement that kept his head straight while those in other districts were losing theirs. He noted many districts were "pink slipping" masses of teachers in their scared reaction. He had not done that or other "silly" things. The mission and the reflective process had helped him to defuse anger, to keep calm and focused on the mission, on the real choices he had, and on the educational impact of various decisions. In this district with these individuals, group reflection is clearly a professional activity yielding important and educationally sound outcomes.

Effects on Me

Janet and I had been considered and considered ourselves to be facilitators—sort of—when the group began. But, by the time "mystery" and "autopilot" were in place, our formal facilitator role diminished considerably. Yes, I "knew" a good deal about reflection, but I, with everyone else, was a member and learner in this particular process. Others told me that I was useful in the group because I asked questions and possessed a set of conceptual frameworks differing from the others'. The superintendent once said something like this: "If I go away from a meeting with one good question, it's worth all the time spent." The question might have been mine or someone else's. What slowly dawned on me was that *I* was a group member too. My participation presented a different perspective for the district administrators, but they presented me with perspectives not available at the university.

In fact, the group experience affected me significantly. The most obvious influence was on my teaching. All along, I had been struck with the idea that this was an unusual group of administrators—they talked about kids, learning, pedagogy, and educational issues *all the time*. The "dispenser of knowledge" secondary teaching metaphor and the continuing discussion of process writing and process math caused me to raise questions about—to reflect upon—what I was doing in the classroom. During one semester, I was teaching the introduction to research course for the doctoral program. It has always been a "different" course because I approach it more as a philosophical, epistemological, comparative paradigm experience than a nuts-and-bolts, "how-to" experience.

Because of my group membership, however, I began to see myself more in the dispenser of knowledge role (I am a former secondary teacher!) than was comfortable. I confronted the issue of trading off the volume of "knowledge" students learned against a personalized, individualized, and experiential understanding of the meaning of research. Because of reflection, I tried to cut down the amount of talk and content I provided—but didn't move to a "how do you feel about it?" approach. I altered assignments starting with a letter in the summer requesting that students read two dissertations, one from each of two research paradigms, before the fall, and asked them to bring in what they thought might be a "doable" dissertation problem to pursue. I wanted personal engagement in learning. Their problem became the central basis for short weekly papers requiring them to think through various aspects of several paradigms while focusing on the same problem. I took the risk to trust them more as learners who would take responsibility for their own learning and to become more of a coach myself. Then, at the start of the class, the 16 students I had thought would show up—a number small enough for a seminar format—turned out to be 26! I gave my attempts at change serious second thoughts but then plunged ahead. I told the students specifically what I was trying and why. I discussed the large number and my questions about whether it would work. Through the semester, I had second thoughts but also remained open in describing to them what I thought was happening. My personal reading was that I had been less successful than in prior years. Then came course evaluations. It had worked! To a person, evaluations were positive in reporting the students had a good command of the basic research conceptions in several paradigms. All through the semester, I had brought questions about my teaching to the reflection group. One further interesting matter:

Two of the principals in the group were students in the research course. We all seemed comfortable in both settings and sets of roles.

Reflecting on Reflection in a Group Context

In this group, I play two roles. The first is group member. I had achieved that; I was accepted as one of the group. The second role is researcher trying to comprehend the big picture, trying to understand group reflection as a process. Because I am a group member, in the normal course of events, I have access only to what happens at meetings as I perceive it and through the objective tape-recorded records. I am not around for interactions that occur among the district administrators outside of the formal meetings but are influenced by our meetings. At several points, the group had stopped to reflect on reflection or to focus directly on our group processes. Several of these occasions preceded my delivery of papers on reflection at professional meetings that involved references to the group. Another occasion was when I posed the question of whether reflection affected handling of the budget crisis. These discussions were useful in gaining a larger perspective on what we were doing together, useful to the whole group, not just me.

As a researcher, however, I decided to attempt a deeper understanding of what this joint reflective venture was producing. To accomplish this, I interviewed each school district member at the year-and-a-half point. (I did not interview Janet because she had taken a semester leave to pursue some work at a university removed from the area, where she has since taken a position.) I believed the group had developed enough trust and had a strong enough set of norms that my interviews, while they would affect individuals and the group, would not seriously bias or skew either what I heard or the continuing process of group reflection. With this understanding, I interviewed each member at her or his workplace for a time ranging from 45 minutes to 2½ hours. I asked three major questions: (a) What does reflection mean to you? (b) What effects had being a member of the group had on your professional and personal life? (c) Had the process affected the district as a whole? The responses were fascinating. What follows is a brief summary of only a part of what I discovered.

Definitions of reflection and our process together contained shared central meanings but were expressed in many different ways. The director of curriculum and pupil services said:

It has the conscious effect of an awareness of wanting to think about what I am doing. . . . What it makes me do is stop a lot during the day and say, "What exactly am I doing?" or "Why did I react to someone in the way I did?" Or if I made a decision without thinking about it a lot, I feel uncomfortable about it. It's an automatic feeling of discomfort. I should have paid more attention to what I was saying. It is becoming a learned behavior, an automatic response to just existing. . . . The group has taught me I can control my own behavior.

Although the language is not the same as our technical terms in the first chapters, she is indicating that the reflective posture is becoming acculturated into her theory-in-use.

The director of language arts and testing used a metaphor:

Reflection is that mirror where the image and the reality at some fine point meet in a pure sense. It is the attempt to get to that point. Reflection is an attempt to get to that reality, that pure descriptive mode, and finding the tool, finding within yourself the route . . . to make some things more conscious, bring them to the frontal lobe. In some respects it has not done what I wanted it to do and in other respects it has done more. What it hasn't done is to give me a particular way to approach situations in a reflective manner. I still tend to react emotionally when I am feeling verbally assaulted. . . . My first reaction still tends to be a bit emotional—although I'm getting better at distancing myself. What it has done is to allow me to peel back a layer on every situation I have been involved in and get to another layer underneath, that and another and another. . . . I see potential in situations I didn't see before.

The three elementary principals had responses clustered around improving performance in their roles. The first statement is from a male principal who joined the group during our second year on a "try two sessions with no obligation" invitation from the superintendent. He remains an active group member.

> The group is comfortable . . . an honest assessment of determining how we can do our individual jobs better. . . . How we are doing it is through any and all professionally and personally related occurrences and events, literature, some sophisticated research brought in—we kind of bounce from how does that fit with a similar experience someone has had that may be personal, how does that tie into the group or to me assessing what I am trying to do in this job. It's done in a way that reduces the hierarchical order, allows us to let our hair down and throw an issue on the table that could be a problem or controversial. It doesn't matter who jumps in. It could be the superintendent or a colleague principal or anyone else. Personally when I leave the meeting I think about the gestalt, about these situations rather than a lot of isolated incidents. A lot of thinking about what we are doing goes on after the meetings. It has broadened the scope of the way I think about what an elementary principal should be doing.

One of the elementary principals reported always being personally and professionally reflective on an individual basis. The group process, however, added dimensions.

> I saw it as extending into the change we are all going through [in the district and in individual schools] so I could be a little more critical and broaden my perspective, come at things from a different angle, listen better, be more tolerant, try to be more understanding. . . . Doing it as a group has broadened the base, given more depth, helped me to be more detached when I need to be detached so I can assess things and probably look at them more objectively, be more open and not get myself into a defensive posture. One of the things that makes our group effective is it covers a lot of buildings and a lot of perspectives and background circumstances and roles.

The third principal described it as

an opportunity to get together in a philosophical group. You don't have time to do that [under normal conditions]. We get involved in how to solve a bus problem, or a parent problem . . . but to really talk at a philosophical level, there's no time for that [normally]. At the initial stages I felt it would help me to get perspective as a principal. I always need perspective. I tend to get caught up in what I am doing. I can lose sight of things, not that I get emotionally involved, but I am not always able to step back, step away from things—and that's important. It gives me perspective and ultimately helps me to ask myself how can I be a better principal, a better educator, help kids better. I'm always looking for that. I'm very serious about that. I don't ever want to become complacent.

The associate superintendent was new to the district the year the group started. He had some prior acquaintance with using literature as a springboard for reflection in a dissertation he had recently completed.

It is a way for us to structure some time in these very busy days to consider what we are doing, the impact it has on the organization and the impact it has on us, and on relationships of us to each other, us to the teaching staff, to the children—although we often don't get to that, we start with that and work our way back. The thing that gets to me most is that we talk about common problems and we get out of the organizational perspective and talk a little more about how we feel about it, how we acted the way we did, how we would act in a different situation or a similar situation. It is different [than the way I thought about reflection previously]. I saw it as a private activity, almost like a meditation at the end of the day or while driving home. What I find extraordinary here is that when you are with other people it opens more avenues because someone mentions something that you may not have been thinking of. Or it will key an idea or an emotion into you that you may not have been thinking or feeling about. The other thing that the group has done for me is that, as a newcomer, it has given me more accessibility to people without their organizational faces on.

This description clearly states the importance of the emotional dimension in the group's work. That theme is also evident in some of the previous statements.

The superintendent gave this description:

As a group process it is collectively examining our assumptions, perceptions, goals, values—almost like working with a scientific team analyzing the reality we are experiencing. On a personal level it is reevaluating and reexamining my belief system, professional belief system, personal belief system, my way of dealing with the world and others—in a nonthreatening manner. I don't feel threatened by the process as we do it. It is self-examination in a way that permits recognition of failure for the purpose of growth—even recognition of strength for the purpose of growth. It has an element of analysis and examination for the purpose of growth that is permeating my work and my life on a personal level. The group is improving its ability to communicate. I suppose I am too, but I am also improving my knowledge of myself and my values. I guess the group is reexamining whether their personal values are in line with the group values, in support of, in conflict with. All those things in this experience are permissible. A person could recognize any of those positions and even describe it and share it with someone else and not have to suffer a consequence for it. In simple terms, for the group, it is an analysis of the value system, perceptions, and the way we communicate for the purpose of growing and doing our jobs better.

Personally, reflection has a professional level which is looking at how I do my work as an educator, an administrator in this setting. Also on a more personal level, what kind of satisfactions I am looking for and whether the cost to achieve them is worth the effort—whether I am getting the results I am after. Am I doing the right thing in the right way—a personal awareness. Then later I see it in communication and the ability to relate and hear what someone else is saying—personal awareness that is growing. . . . The metaphors and the examination of them has put me on a very different level of awareness. It has changed how I use metaphors. I think a long time about how the audience will receive and perceive a metaphor now whereas before I didn't.

That level of awareness is unique. . . . Things that I used to assume—I assume less now. Looking at change—does it come by pushing others or by changing your own behaviors? What behaviors do you control? Isn't changing your own behaviors going to produce a bigger effect than trying to make them change? The conflict and change discussions have been very important to me.

The superintendent's description makes very clear a point that all others brought up in their interviews. The reflective process as we are experiencing it in a group has both individual and corporate dimensions. All of the members at some point described themselves as having been personally introspective or reflective throughout their lives. The director of language arts had been keeping a formal journal since 1984. The superintendent went back to undergraduate days and the value of the humanities for examining one's life. What all reported, however, was that the group experience added an important and powerful dimension they had not experienced before, a dimension affecting both the individual members and their work together as an educational and administrative team.

I got solid answers to some of the questions that had engaged me in the quest in the first place. Yes, the intact work group experience was important. Yes, it could work. Yes, role and power positions could more or less be hung like hats on a rack before individuals entered the room for a reflective session. No, there did not have to be fear of openness or negative repercussions for providing honest, unfiltered information as problems and issues were confronted. Yes, there was a multiplier effect that did not obtain when groups were composed of individuals from disparate workplaces. Mystery took on new meaning as I came to understand the personal perspectives of other actors in the drama we are creating together. Mystery was neat stuff for everyone involved.

The definitions of reflection themselves began to answer the second and third questions about individual and district effects of reflection. Large portions of the interviews were catalogues of attributions of important effects of the reflective process and detailed stories to support them. Space permits only a brief indication of the interview contents.

Individual effects ranged from general to very specific. The superintendent reported a reduction in anger; others indicated the same sense. This came with the "distancing" and the "standing back," the analysis and reflection of experiential learning. All agreed the group process had significantly reduced administrative isolation. They reported increased sensitivity to a number of issues: power and its use, the relatively disadvantaged position of parents approaching the school, the effects on one's behavior and the awareness that there were other choices in the way we act, the importance of clear, unfiltered, honest communication. One principal gave a detailed report of working with student discipline in a totally different way as a result of group participation. The new was working much better than the old way. He was excited. Almost all reported an increased ability and sensitivity to listening, to trying to understand the perspectives of others, to getting more broadly based information before coming to important decisions, to reacting less defensively and emotionally to kinds of situations that in the past might have been seen as more personally threatening. The associate superintendent described the surprise he experienced during one school board meeting when a patron attacked something the district was doing. Instead of reacting defensively, the superintendent asked him for any suggestions he might be able to provide for improving response to the problem. Suggestions would be appreciated and taken into careful consideration. The superintendent's open request had been honest and was not expected. It both defused the attack and provided the opportunity for increasing the pool of information for decision making if, in fact, the individual had information to provide.

SERENDIPITY STRIKES AGAIN

I am confronted with more important data and more interesting stories about the positive individual and districtwide effects of the reflective process than I can possibly recount. But, in reviewing the tapes, serendipity struck again. My interview with the superintendent was interrupted by a phone call from a principal who is not in the group. He was on the phone 7 or 8 minutes, mostly listening and saying, "uhuh, uhuh," to indicate so. The whole time he was writing very rapid and complete notes. When we resumed the interview, he made continuous reference to the call in indicating how the reflective process had enabled him to handle it differently than he would have a year before. What I had captured on tape was a spontaneous reflection session in which both reflection-on-action and reflection-in-action are evident.

I have chosen to give the complete conversation in the original voices, his and mine. Doing so is a trade-off against fascinating accounts in other voices. In addition to the spontaneity and clear authenticity of this conversation, which included numerous long pauses for thought, it indicates in condensed form both individual and district effects of the reflective process. And, while the conversation concerns mostly one other administrator, it is readily apparent how the changing thinking and behaviors of the superintendent were likely affecting the whole school district. Further, there is a clear correspondence between the discussion of the call and the superintendent's platform (see Figure 7.1).

Superintendent: I was listening to stories about past divorces and child abuse, maybe 25 years of background for one incident, but it was important to this principal that I had the whole picture before he hung up. In my previous approach to things he said to me things like, "This is elementary school and these things are important here." And I said, "Of course, I recognize that, and I'm willing to listen." What I was really doing just then was letting him know that I had confidence that everything he had to say was valuable and that I was appreciating his willingness to share. Even if I don't use the information, he is preparing me for the next event that I am going to have to go through.

Me: You were, however, writing furiously.

Superintendent: Right. I was taking those notes so that if I wanted to reiterate . . . what I would have done is given him back a lot of what he had told me so that I communicated to him that I had taken it down. [long pause] This reflective process has taught me to go at my job with each person where that person is coming from not where I am coming from. We were in a meeting; that was an interruption. I could have said to him, "Could you call back?" It's already well beyond his normal day. "Could you call in the morning?" Any of the normal bureaucratic responses he could have gotten. I might have given him that. But the reflective process has caused me to reflect on those responses and say, "Why?" "Why do that now?" And weigh all those things and also know that I am responding to my own need to control my time and not his need to get information to me and to get some corroboration that what he did was OK, or approved of, or supported. Now he can go home and feel that he has done all the things he should have done, and he doesn't have a superintendent who is going to be after him tomorrow because of some phone call that followed later in the evening. So all of those things I think happened because of the reflective process. . . . He is not in the group, but he's getting the same kind of treatment the group gets, which I think is a powerful carryover. Which I would say surprised me. Before the holidays if you had asked me, "Do you treat people outside the group differently than you treat people inside the group?" I would have said, "Yes." Now I would say, "No, not that differently." Some of them will treat me different, but I don't look at them differently.

Me: What's happened?

Superintendent: It's just a longer period of reflection. More practice, more application of the learning process that I'm going through.

Me: Is it more risky to do that with them now?

Superintendent: No. Because we have done this [reflection], I would say it is less risky in all my behaviors.

Me: Earlier on you might have differentiated on risk, inside/outside of the group, something like that?

Superintendent: Right. Definitely, I would differentiate on how much a risk it was to have these type of behaviors we have within the reflective group shared with other people who are not within the group. Today, I find that those reflective behaviors are helpful every place, with everyone I work with.

Me: You haven't gotten burned?

Superintendent: No! Not at all. And even if I do, it won't be because of the reflective behaviors necessarily. Those behaviors are making it easier for me to do my work. And as I extend it to others, I'm doing better at it.

Me: How do you know that?

Superintendent: The results I'm getting. Just that kind of conversation I just had. A year ago he would probably have hung up angry, demanded that I support him. It would have been a totally different type of conversation: "This is what happened. She accused me of not telling the truth and covering up. I demand your support!" I didn't have any of that just now.

Me: Prior to this was there some history of him not being defended or something?

Superintendent: I might have asked him "Why?" at some point in the conversation.

Me: Nothing like having betrayed him in the past?

Superintendent: No, no.

Me: It was just a set of assumptions, just business being delivered as usual.

Superintendent: Right. The question I might have asked might have incited him. Now I just avoided the question.

Me: I was listening. You just said, "uhuh, uhuh, uhuh." Would you have written as much before?

Superintendent: No.

Me: Does that in itself focus you?

Superintendent: Yes it does. It gives me the opportunity to evaluate the whole picture and the pieces. And I don't need to make a decision right now. I don't need all the information. He was giving me a lot of information. I don't need the reasons behind it to know what my next step is, whereas before I would look for the reasons behind things. They are not always known. That is one of the things that reflection has brought out. The reasons are not always known and when you ask him "Why?" you put him on the defensive. So I try to avoid that question. My last question to him was, "You believe that I will be getting a phone call now from this person?" He responded, "Yes, and she'll be irate and probably not want to accept any of the things that I told her." Then I replayed a little bit of the conversation and said, "Fine, I know what to do, thank you very much. I appreciate that you took the time." So, I didn't incite any defensive behaviors in him, I don't think. I still have a confident, capable principal who is coming to work tomorrow morning. He will deal with his problems much better tomorrow, and I will not have created more problems for him.

Me: What you may also have done through that incident is created a better relationship.

Superintendent: Yes.

Me: Does he know that you are changing?

Superintendent: Yes, I believe he does. He would probably call it maturation in the job. He might call it a natural development. Basically he likes me on certain levels as an educator. I think that he is pleased that our relationship is progressing along positive veins. He probably thinks that he has been a big help to me in this process of growth for me. And I would say in some ways he has been a big help because he has been one of my biggest challenges for growth, for me personally.

Me: He's produced real stuff to work on.

Superintendent: Right! At the same time, as I change my behaviors he offers me insight or follow-up that confirms that what I am doing or attempting to do is working—at least in our work that we share. . . . [pause] The other things that have happened is that I have learned to examine the level of patience I have with others. Now I ask questions that I guess superintendents frequently fail to ask someone else. I have asked some of my immediate associates here. We have been in a situation where we have a difficult path to pursue, and we have people who don't want to go that route and who are very difficult to deal with. "Do you believe that I should behave differently in that situation?" "Do you think I was too patient?" There is a point at which some leadership must be confrontational too. Confrontation used to come easily to me. And it was a weakness in many instances. So I have had to learn to do some of the other things.

Me: The jury affirms that you are doing better on patience.

Superintendent: [laughter] Is that right? I'm working on it, Robert!

Me: The jury sees it and they like it.

Superintendent: On the other hand, I am sure there a people who would like to see the superintendent say: "You, change or get out!" However, that can't be done. Getting out isn't an option. You can't tell a person either/or. What you learn on the job is that there are no either/or's. There are degrees of either this or either that. [pause] I call it ambiguities. The ambiguities we deal with at work (which are probably the most important elements in the long run for effectiveness) I now share with people—frequently—which I didn't do before. I take assessments more frequently of those ambiguities, unclear pathways.

Me: Beyond just the group here?

Superintendent: Yes.

Me: So the behavior is spilling over?

Superintendent: Right. I'm picking up a lot more information. I'm getting better insight. I'm taking longer to select a pathway. And I think we're getting better cooperation.

SUMMING UP

The "experiment" in group reflection is continuing and the junior high principal has joined us. All of us are convinced of its utility and are content to follow "mystery" wherever it takes us. The university and the school district have filed a joint federal grant proposal to extend group reflection to teachers, a 3-year project if funded. We are also submitting proposals for presentations at professional meetings. Further, I will spend part of a coming semester of academic leave in the district doing broader ethnographic work, attempting to understand the impacts of our work from a perspective broader than the core group, and shadowing the members of the group in their daily work.

I have learned things important to others who for the purpose of individual and organizational development wish to engage in reflection in intact work groups. When this group began, I had already developed the concept of "buffering." Because reflective practice needs a Model II environment and because Model I environments predominate in organizations, successful nurturing of reflective practice requires a buffer to protect those attempting to reflect from typical organizational norms and culture. "Business as usual" as we call it, must be buffered against. Anyone, anywhere in the hierarchy, *may* serve as a buffer, but only for those below on the organizational ladder. So a principal has the potential to buffer her teachers, a teacher his students. Not that buffering is easy! It always means going against the tide.

In the reflection group, the superintendent buffers everyone in the district, knowingly and with full intent. Because he wants to grow personally through reflection and wants his colleagues to grow and his district to improve its educational program through reflection, and because he took risks, was open, and modeled behaviors that spring from Model II assumptions, the process took off successfully. He is at the organizational apex, and it makes a big difference. He buffers everyone in the district, makes it permissible and desirable to engage in reflection. That the process has been as successful as it has been is in large part attributable to him, both as an individual who values growth through what we are doing and as the apex person in the district. Had he not been 100% in favor of the undertaking— really in this case out in front leading it through modeling of behavior—I would not be writing the story I am. Had the same man occupied the office of associate superintendent, director, or principal in a district with a superintendent either opposed to reflection or indifferent to it, my guess is that the process would not have had nearly the personal and systemic effects it has had. Buffering from the apex makes a great deal of difference. It would be very difficult to develop a culture of reflection in a district or school where the leadership is against it or not passionately supportive.

I have learned about the role of facilitator in such a group through experience. While I exerted more formal facilitator behavior in the beginning than I do now, my authority and decisional scope was always less than when I facilitate a university course or a PDC group. While it is more subtle and anything but "in charge," through the associate superintendent's comments I have come to appreciate the special role of facilitator in such a group. He noted that, regardless of Janet's or my behavior (which are not unimportant), we are the symbolic embodiment of permission to act in ways other than "business as usual." When we are present, it's OK to be philosophical, to set no agenda, to explore without having to come to conclusion, to operate by different norms, to leave roles hanging outside the door. Perhaps this is an illustration of the old proverb about being 50 miles from home to be considered an expert. I am not thoroughly convinced I could facilitate a reflection group in my own place of work. My guess is that an "outside" facilitator would greatly increase the probabilities of success in most settings.

The skills and orientations needed to facilitate in such a group do not differ from those outlined in Chapters 3, 5, and 6. In this case, group members were already quite mature in their communication and group process skills. I did not have to provide "instruction" in these in the way I do in my course. The other things I am specifically aware of is raising the concrete issues of discussion to a more general plane at the end of sessions and using my academic conceptual capital to frame issues in a slightly different light. These were often accomplished through asking questions. All my skills and knowledge were no doubt useful and employed from time to time, but I was less aware of them and provided considerably less "leadership" as compared with that provided in other settings. What facilitators need to do in other attempts to build such groups will be context specific.

The final issue is that I am convinced reflective practice has the potential to be a very powerful vehicle for organizational as well as individual change and development. At our last reflection meeting, I asked for response to a draft of the first part of this chapter. Was it too great a claim to say that reflection may produce school reform? The question sparked a lively conversation. The superintendent's reaction was that *reform* is not strong enough. Reflection does more than reform. It fosters nothing short of "systemic change." I can live with that assessment very easily with a caveat concerning buffering from the apex.

It is clear the culture of the district is changing. It is changing because individuals are changing, individuals who are first and foremost competent and committed educators, individuals who want to grow and improve themselves, individuals who are leaders in strategic positions within the district and within school buildings. It is a "quiet" change process, coming about as they change themselves, as they think, feel, and act differently. Changing themselves alters how others respond to them. As they work in concert and support each other, the individual changes have a multiplier effect that in small and large ways reverberate through the social and cultural system of the schools and the district. It is a quiet change without grand announcements, special programs, or large expenditures. It is just a group of dedicated individuals who have decided to look carefully at what we do and how we might make it better. It is working. Whether it can work in other places, and whether it takes a very special set of circumstances and talented individuals, are questions that remain unanswered but need answering. We call on our readers to take heart, take a few risks, give it a good try, and help us to come up with some solid answers. It seems there is tremendous potential in this individual as well as situation- and context-specific approach to improving education. Reflective practice draws on and enhances the most important and prevalent resource education has: human resources. There is great hope here, something worth investing energy in pursuing.

8 An Empowering Process

Earlier chapters outlined the conceptual and practical framework for reflective practice. Nonetheless, there are neither pat formulas nor one best approach. To the contrary, as the narratives in Chapters 5, 6, and 7 demonstrate, reflective practice takes many different forms depending on factors such as setting, time framework, context, participants' characteristics and objectives, and the personality of the facilitator.

Among our narratives, for example, the situations differ on dimensions of time, focus, setting, and personal choice. "The Reflective Administrator" course is offered within the confines of the academic semester. The reflective practice seminar for high school principals extended over a 3-month period as part of a full-time program. The administrative reflection group has met regularly for 2 years and will continue in the coming year.

In "The Reflective Administrator" course, prospective administrators explore the concepts of reflective practice and their own espoused theories and theories-in-use as professional educators engaged in a variety of different roles. In the principal renewal program, principals used this insulated time and space to examine and improve their administrative practice. In the administrative reflection group, the superintendent, central office administrators, and principals examined educational issues that were important to them individually and collectively to improve personal practice and district effectiveness.

Another important dimension distinguishing reflective practice is choice. Usually, individuals who engage in reflective practice do so out of choice, but to varying degrees. At one end of the continuum, Kottkamp was invited to visit the district—an invitation that extended into a long-term commitment. Accordingly, his role as facilitator was highly nondirective. At the other end of the continuum, Osterman facilitated the principal renewal program, where principals had little choice regarding their participation. For two of the principals, the choice was to participate or lose their positions, and, although their personal control was respected within the context of the program, unlike those teachers and administrators who knowingly entered a reflective practice situation, they were not informed about the specific nature of the seminar prior to their entry.

By highlighting the differences among these situations, we also highlight the essential similarities. By describing our personal experiences in these different situations and settings, we hoped to explain in meaningful ways what reflective practice is like from the perspective of facilitator and participant, how it unfolds in varying and often unpredictable ways.

The narratives serve another purpose as well. In the first two chapters, we argue that reflective practice is a viable and effective means of professional development that leads to change on a personal and organizational basis. There is no shortage of writings that espouse the value of reflective practice, but there is less information that documents this relationship. The three narrative accounts we wrote join a relatively small but growing list of presentations, articles, and research reports—many reported here—regarding the nature and efficacy of reflective practice methods. Despite the many variations, despite the differences in facilitators, attitudes of participants, context, or length of the process, reflective practice seems to have a far greater impact on people's lives than other learning experiences. As Francine Minnick, a second-grade teacher in the Teacher Development and Organizational Change (TDOC) project, explained: "The process . . ., with reflection at the heart of it, proved to be one of the most significant learning experiences and change agents in my nineteen years as an educator" (Berkey et al., 1990, p. 220).

Practitioners who engage in reflective practice give similar reports about the way the process has affected them, and the changes they describe are both personal and organizational. First, they talk about a changing view of the world and seeing things in new and different ways. They talk about changes in their attitudes and beliefs and about new meaning. Second, they talk about changes in their practice, how even well into their careers they are changing the way they do things. Third, they talk about how the nature of their relationships with professional colleagues is changing, how they are seeing themselves as part of supportive teams with shared goals and values rather than as isolated individuals struggling in an uncaring environment.

Given the consistencies in these reports, it would be difficult to deny that the reflective process stimulates a process culminating in behavioral change. But why? What in the process enables people to reconsider long-held beliefs and to break patterns of behavior reinforced by habit and culture? Although this question could result in a very complex answer, there are clearly two aspects of the process that are particularly supportive of professional growth and development. The first is articulation of core beliefs and values; the second is an informative, supportive, and collaborative communication process.

ARTICULATION OF CORE BELIEFS AND VALUES

To differing degrees, reflective practice strategies encourage articulation of personal educational beliefs in general or context-specific ways. Typically, what seems a simple task—to describe personally held professional beliefs and values—proves to be surprisingly difficult. When asked to prepare an administrative platform, for example, it's not uncommon for educators to comment that they've never really thought about what they believe and to describe the intense effort required to complete the task. Nonetheless, they find the process revealing and stimulating. One principal described the experience of preparing a mission statement this way:

> When you made me sit down and write a vision, I realized that I was functioning on political beliefs that I hadn't really thought about that seriously. I believed that children who didn't speak English needed a bilingual program and for 6-8 years of my life, I focused on that. So the vision statement made me really think—what do you believe about education, what do you believe a school should be, in *all* respects—and then also to take a look at what I had done in education and at what I had failed to do in education.

When the mission or vision is clear, a number of things happen. The discrepancies—the contradictions between what we say and what we do—become more obvious, and the contrast between the vision and the reality becomes an incentive to take action (Senge, 1990). As Teresa Curtis, a teacher in the TDOC project, explained: "Why were we willing to make commitments and why were we willing to take risks? It was because we cared about closing that gap between the reality that we saw in the classroom and the idea that we could envision" (Berkey et al., 1990, p. 216).

With a clearly defined purpose, it becomes easier to develop a sense of focus and to establish priorities more clearly. In Chapter 6, John describes how he spent so much energy and time putting out the fires that he never really thought about where he was going. Later, with his vision more clearly defined, he found it easier to decide which fires needed to be fought: "If it's not that serious, treat it as not that serious and focus your energies on something that is important."

The clarification process also affects the nature of interaction with colleagues. Blase and Kirby (1992), for example, demonstrated the importance of explicit values in empowering or transformational leadership. They found that principals seen as most effective are those demonstrating consistency between their expectations and actions: They act in ways consistent with their beliefs. In contrast, principals less clear in their convictions and less consistent in their actions emit inconsistent messages and lead teachers "to be guarded and protective, afraid to trust the unpredictable" (p. 109). It was evident from the data given by the superintendent in the administrative reflection group that, as his behaviors became more predictable and in line with his espousals, his subordinates' perceptions of him became more positive.

The process of articulating values and beliefs and exploring practice enhances a sense of personal responsibility for one's own actions. Abby, one of the principals in the renewal program, explained the effects of articulation in this way: "I loved not being clear, I loved the ambiguity . . . because you could never hold yourself responsible. That's an understanding I've come to: if things are really not that clear, there's nothing I can do about it so then I can't be responsible."

A great deal has been written about the importance of vision for leadership. Beginning with the effective schools research and the importance of expectations in shaping a culture of achievement, educational and organizational researchers have highlighted the importance of clearly defined values, beliefs, and goals (Leithwood & Jantzi, 1990; Peters & Waterman, 1982; Senge, 1990; Sergiovanni, 1991). The articulation of values, beliefs, and goals—the development of vision—is central to reflective practice. At every stage, the individual examines his or her personal beliefs within the organizational context. What is it that I want to accomplish? What are my beliefs about good schools and what facilitates learning? What are the implications for the way I should act?

Through articulating a platform, the individual begins to see the self in a different perspective. Where before the "system" may have been the dominant figure, now the individual emerges from the background as focal. The emphasis is no longer system constraints but individual options. DeCharms's (1968, 1976, 1984) concept of *origin/ pawn* is useful here in explaining how the "origin" functions within the context of organizational constraints. For the "pawn," all individual actions are shaped by beliefs about what the "system" will allow. In contrast, the origin, working among constraints no less real, merely shifts the focus to determine what she or he would like to do given the environmental restrictions. The organization hasn't changed, but the individual has refocused the lens to construct a different reality.

Reflective practice enables us to experience ourselves as origins within educational settings.

COMMUNICATION

Reflective practice thrives in an environment of open communication: People speak freely to one another about their ideas, concerns, successes, and failures. Because there is so much conversation, so much interaction, and, because most of it focuses on professional work issues, the reflective practice environment—whether a small group of teachers, or administrators, or an entire school—becomes a learning environment. Reflective practitioners focus on their own work in an effort to develop a deeper understanding and a higher level of competence, and, as they share ideas and information, they increase their sense of efficacy and effectiveness. All of these inter-related aspects of enhanced work-related communication are clearly in evidence throughout the district in which key administrators meet regularly to continue their reflective conversations. They are also reported in other narratives and studies about reflective practice environments (Berkey et al., 1990; Sagor, 1991).

The flow of information in the process of reflective practice is very different than what most professionals encounter in their organizations: People pursuing reflective practice have access to more information and different information. In reflective practice settings, the communication process is designed to give participants a great deal of information—or feedback—about their own performance. This access to information, this openness of communication about one another's work, is very different in many ways than typical organizational communication. Although performance feedback is a critical element in professional growth, it is a rare organization in which individuals actually have access to *meaningful* feedback about their own work. Feedback is offered infrequently and, when it is provided, it is often unrelated to the needs or interests of the practitioners. In most organizations, formal evaluations provide one of the few opportunities for professionals to obtain information about their performance, yet we know that even the evaluation process seldom yields information about performance helpful to the recipient.

Feedback offered in the reflective practice context is different in several important from that which professionals typically receive. In this book and within the framework of reflective practice, performance feedback is not viewed as evaluative in the sense that performance is observed and then assessed according to criteria established by organizational superiors. Within reflective practice, performance feedback is not evaluative but informative. It is not prescriptive but descriptive. Information is provided for the practitioner to make appropriate decisions and choices about his or her own professional progress. Because the facilitator and other members of the group avoid the role of evaluator and prescriber, the locus of control remains with the practitioner.

Studies of evaluation demonstrate that a major problem with evaluation as it is typically practiced is that performance feedback is often unrelated to actual performance. Teachers frequently receive written evaluations indicating that the supervisor failed to understand their actions as they were intended or they receive evaluations based only on a portion of their performance. Consequently, teachers do not feel that the supervisor understands or appreciates their work, and it is unlikely that supervisor/supervisee interaction will lead to professional dialogue or growth. In these situations, problems occur for two reasons: (a) The supervisor is offering his or her assessment *of* performance rather than information *about* performance and (b) the information offered is privately and unilaterally given rather than shared in a collaborative and dialogic process.

Within the reflective practice model, providing feedback is a very different process. Practitioners receive a different kind of information; the information is generated in a different way; and the interpretation of information takes place in an open and equitable discussion among all the relevant parties. In reflective practice, the facilitator is not a superior assessing performance quality but a collaborator stimulating professional growth in a way consistent with the needs of the individual.

Our ability to engage in reflective practice and to share performance information openly with one another is colored by our beliefs that professionals need and want more information and are able to discuss problems in an open way with colleagues. While it is not too difficult to accept the idea of providing positive feedback about successful effort, it is much more difficult to believe that professionals want to know where and when their performance is less than perfect. Yet, the experience of reflective practitioners as well as a substantial body of research supports the position that individuals need, want, value, and use information about their performance even when the information highlights problems. Although Schon (1983) talked about how reflective practice requires the practitioner to "give up the rewards of unquestioned authority, the freedom to practice without challenge to competence, the comfort of relative invulnerability, and the gratifications of deference" (p. 299), the experience of reflective practitioners suggests that these "rewards" are more likely to be a burden compared with the satisfactions derived from honest and open communication. In her work with a group of therapists, for example, Mattingly (1991) reported that "nearly everyone mentioned their relief at being able to speak of their practice as a place where things often did not run smoothly and where they and their patients often did not seem to agree about what should happen in therapy" (p. 254). Principals in the renewal program described their surprise at seeing business leaders as well as other principals struggling with problems similar to their own. This discovery that others don't have all the answers was liberating and led not to a sense of complacency but to a renewed search for answers. The district superintendent is learning that it is less risky to communicate with everyone the way he communicates with those inside the reflection group than to treat them differently.

Reflective practice breaks the typical conspiracy of silence; it takes the onus away from problems. It requires that problems be viewed objectively, not judgmentally. This simple distinction is extremely difficult and extremely important. It requires that we say honestly, "Here is a problem that may need attention" rather than "Here is a problem resulting from your incompetence." What requires attention is not only the language but the underlying assumption.

The process of reflective practice not only ensures that professionals have access to a growing body of information about their performance, it also ensures that the information is provided in a way that fosters learning. Blase and Kirby (1992) found that effective principals visited classrooms and usually provided feedback to teachers after their visits. Teachers found this practice effective and acceptable "because it was accompanied by genuine interest and support. It was not viewed as obtrusive or punitive. Instead, teachers associated it with opportunities for improvement" (p. 108). Although anxiety levels went up a bit, teachers reported that they worked harder, were more innovative, and felt better about their own performance. Chances are that, if researchers looked at the kind of feedback these principals provided, they would find that the information was descriptive rather than prescriptive.

Another story illustrates the impact of descriptive feedback. In the principal renewal program, interim progress reports were required. To minimize the potential negative impact of this process, the facilitator established the following conditions: (a) A single progress report would be prepared for the group and would be shared internally with all the principals and the project adviser; (b) the report would not be released to the principals' district supervisors; (c) the reports would include descriptive information only, that is, reports of session activities. Preparing the first report tested the facilitator's own Model II beliefs. Much of Abby's behavior in class had been obstructive: Should it be described or not? Should the report only include the positive growth and overlook the problem spots? The Model II assumptions won out, and the report included the negatives as well as the positives. While describing the principal's intellectual engagement with new ideas and approaches, the report also commented on the gap between her theory and practice by noting the continued use of critical and abrasive language and its inflammatory impact on the group.

In the session following the receipt of this report, the principals wanted to discuss it. Abby opened the conversation by talking about how she was not always perceived as she really was (even though she had described herself almost word for word in the same way in a previous meeting). At this point, for the first time, she began to talk about what she did and why she did it. For the first time, she addressed deep-seated feelings that led her to remain aloof and isolated.

At a later point in the discussion, in response to the facilitator's concern about confronting her with the information, she commented that, had the information not been included, she would have known that the facilitator was a liar and never would have trusted her again. In this instance, the feedback had a positive impact: It stimulated thought, discussion, and further engendered openness and trust among the participants. But it is important to remember a few preconditions. There was already a climate of openness established within the group: Individuals could express their feelings openly as long as they followed the conversational guidelines ensuring that individuals would neither dominate the discussion nor engage in criticizing or blaming. It was also clear that problems were acceptable and could be discussed openly and without recrimination. In addition, because there was open communication, there was nothing in the report that had not already been observed and discussed within the context of the group. If anything, the progress report was not so much the observations of an outside observer as a written statement of the group's own discussions and observations. There was no question that the data were valid. Presentation in written form, however, reframed the data and gave them more power.

This open flow of communication about professional issues has a number of positive effects. According to Senge (1990), providing people with information about performance enables them to develop a better picture of the current reality. The contrast between what is and what we would like, the contrast between the reality and the vision, he maintains, is the source of the creative tension essential to personal and organizational growth. Through the reflective process, individuals become more aware of these discrepancies; they also become more aware of their own roles. As people have more information about their practice, they are better able to identify ways they can improve their own performance and are more likely to take action.

Through reflective practice, individuals learn about their own performance. Because of the emphasis on exploration, analysis, and collaboration, individuals also have access to more information about alternative strategies. The process of reflective practice expands the pool of resources available to any individual. By bringing more people into the process, it also provides multiple perspectives. In the interviews with the administrators in the districtwide reflection group, every one of them independently reported the important benefit of the multiple perspectives they obtained from reflecting collaboratively as opposed to the individual reflections many of them had conducted throughout their adult lives.

School personnel—teachers and administrators—work in very isolated ways within their districts and buildings. Teachers are bounded by their classrooms or departments and have few opportunities for collegial discussion, let alone focused discussions about their work. Administrators too—principals and superintendents alike—lead lonely existences meeting infrequently for professional conversations with their colleagues. Reflective practice expands the dialogue and provides a structure in which colleagues can share information and ideas. This alone is a valuable improvement; but, in some cases, the pool of resources expands even more with the involvement of an outside facilitator such as the university researcher. The importance of these different perspectives in stimulating change was explained by Teresa Curtis, a first-grade teacher in the TDOC project:

> I have taught for seventeen years, worked hard, and tried to be a good teacher. My colleagues and I had gone to inservices and workshops and read professional journals. We had been very open to trying new ideas, and yet we had not made many of these changes. I believe that the reason the outside stimulus is necessary is that the culture of the situation that teachers are in is so ingrained. A totally different, fresh perspective can trigger new ideas. (Berkey et al., 1990, p. 216)

Reflective practice affects individuals and their organizations in another way. The open and descriptive flow of communication creates a climate of caring and collaboration and helps to create partnerships that can cut across administrative lines (Barnett, 1990). Likert (1961), for example, was one of the early theorists who emphasized the importance of interaction and influence among members and leaders in organizations: When an individual is involved with others, he or she is more fully implicated as a person, more committed, more involved. When people talk to one another, they are more likely to like one another (Homans, 1950). The more they like and care about each other, the harder they will work to ensure team success. Confirming this perspective, one of the teachers in the Washington project reported: "It's been exhausting but fun because of the relationships, collaboration, and support" (Sagor, 1991). Similar feelings were described by a teachers in the TDOC project (Berkey et al., 1990):

> Collaboration provided us with an opportunity to learn more as a group of people than we could as individuals. We knew that as a community of learners, we would be more motivated, stimulated, and energized with each other. Collaboration also removed the isolation that we felt as classroom teachers, and it removed the isolation that the researchers had from the schools. It lessened some of the anxiety, stress, and frustration. We experienced more cooperation, choice, and autonomy. We began to tap into each other's energy and to develop mutually beneficial relationships. (p. 216)

EMPOWERMENT

Those who participate in reflective practice often describe a feeling of empowerment. For Minnick, the process has the power to restore one's professionalism and pride in being a teacher (Berkey et al., 1990). Zietlow, another teacher in the project, explained the impact of the process in this way:

> I gained so much confidence in myself, and I learned to respect myself as a professional and to trust my knowledge, that I have the courage to take risks, to try new things, and to be vulnerable. I no longer need to strive to be someone else's ideal model of a teacher, but I can strive to be the best teacher I can be. I can be myself in my classroom now, and my students know they are accepted for themselves. Not only has reflection been powerful in my growth, but as I took that same attitude into my classroom, I saw significant changes in my students' attitudes about

themselves and their learning. When they recognize they are in a safe, non-threatening learning environment, they are much more comfortable to take risks and meet challenges. They take a more active role in their education—contributing to, and even initiating, units of study. (p. 220)

According to theorists Connell and Wellborn (1989), individuals have basic motivational needs to experience competence, autonomy, and relatedness. As students, teachers, or administrators, individuals need to experience themselves as capable of producing desired outcomes and avoiding negative outcomes; they need to feel competent. They also need autonomy, which grows out of the experience of connectedness between one's actions, personal goals, and values as well as control over one's activities. Finally, people need to feel securely connected to the social surroundings and need to experience themselves as worthy and capable of love and respect.

The process of reflective practice responds to each of these motivational needs. It provides the information needed for people to effect positive changes in performance; it respects the right of individuals to exercise self-direction and, in fact, enhances their ability to exercise control over their own actions. Finally, it engages people in a collaborative process of professional development that responds to their needs for relatedness and increases their sense of efficacy.

In sum, reflective practice is an empowering and motivational process because it responds to basic human needs for competence, autonomy, and relatedness. The central reflective processes of communication and collaboration are empowering: They enable individuals to be more effective, to assume greater responsibility for their own performance, and to engage more closely and more productively with others in the workplace. When individuals are more effective, they enable organizations to be more effective.

REFLECTIVE PRACTICE IN AN AGE OF REFORM: A CAVEAT

In Chapter 1, we posed the hypothesis that reflective practice is a viable means to school reform. This statement, however, should not be viewed as simplistic or overly idealistic. Obviously, organizational change, and school reform in particular, is an extremely complex phenomenon. Nonetheless, the chances for success increase to the extent that there are multiple perspectives and a variety of strategies (Bolman & Deal, 1991). Reflective practice is a human resource strategy. Sorely missing from discussions of school reform, this theoretical perspective maintains that organizations and people depend on one another and that processes that satisfy human needs also serve organizational needs. Reflective practice is a process that empowers and motivates individuals and groups through an ongoing process of professional development. In this process, as people begin to envision new possibilities and to work together in different ways to achieve newly defined goals, the possibility of change on a broader level becomes more real.

Reflective practice creates a sense of optimism about organizational change, a sense that change *is* possible. Unlike national and state efforts to achieve school reform through federal funding, revised certification standards, and standardized testing, however, reflective practice is a grass-roots approach to change: Schools will become better places when teachers in classrooms and principals in schools and superintendents in districts begin to talk more about the vision and the reality and when they begin to work together to devise better and more appropriate ways to meet the needs of the children they serve.

Thus reflective practice is empowering at both the individual and the organizational levels; it is a powerful, multilevel source for individual and systemic change. But we are using *empowerment* in a particular way. *Empowerment* is a buzzword, and, in general conversation, especially among persons who think in traditional hierarchical terms, it is often assumed to be something "given to" subordinates, something controlled by superiors and parceled out to subordinates in specific amounts, as in the following: "We empower teachers to make decisions about curriculum and class assignment but, by implication, not about budgets and personnel decisions." This is not our understanding of *empowerment*. As already illustrated by statements from educators, it is not something given but something that emanates from the self. It is not an entity distributed through a chain of command but a willingness and drive to act professionally and responsibly, grounded in a sense of self-esteem, competence, and autonomy. Reflective practice is a major vehicle for empowerment as we conceptualize it, but it is antithetical to the concept of empowerment as a distributable resource.

The caveat concerning reflective practice and school reform is that precisely controlled and externally prescribed reform outcomes simply cannot be achieved through this process. We cannot mandate highly specific reform outcomes of the kinds that state legislatures and departments of education have propounded in recent times. We cannot specify reflection as the means for introducing or changing a particular program, a particular curriculum, or a particular disciplinary procedure. We cannot reach an externally produced, preordained end through genuine reflective practice processes. Because reflective practice leads individuals to improve their own performance, the process ultimately enriches the organization's ability to achieve goals, but it is an unwritten assumption that through reflection many alternative and effective paths to the same goal will emerge.

Whereas the recent social science-oriented thinking in administration placed great emphasis on systems and mid- and macro-level theories that resulted in an impersonal view of the way things work, reflective practice takes a very personal view in placing central importance on individual responsibility and action. It is not that the former emphasis was intended to reduce the importance of the individual, but the kind of thinking and believing it engendered tended to produce that result. Reflective practice does not reject mid- and macro-level social science theories of organizations but removes them from the position of the beginning and end of thinking about improving practice and organizations. In the reflective practice orientation, these conceptual products are grasped and applied when they are useful in solving particular problems, but the problems are identified through the context-specific and idiosyncratic process of individual and collaborative reflection.

This is not to say that reflective practice leads in no predictable direction. In fact, changes brought through reflection will predictably move individuals and organizations toward Model II and away from Model I assumptions and behaviors in a broad way. In a sense, reflective practice not only directs but deflects. As it moves us toward the development of thoughtful and collaborative learning communities, it moves us away from those Model I aspects of organizational behavior that generate defensiveness, isolation, powerlessness, and alienation. It moves us away from unilateral imposition of power, strict externally controlled accountability mechanisms, competition that pits colleagues against one another—all organizational realities that characterize so many of the reform attempts during the past decade. Reflective practice cannot be used to sustain the status quo. If reflective practice operates out of a Model II theory-in-use, it cannot be used to achieve Model I behaviors and ends, just as the commonly used Model I theory-in-use will not result in Model II ends.

Reflective practice is a potentially powerful avenue for school improvement and systemic change. We say "potentially" because it has not been tried yet in any serious way. To try it seriously means calling off "business as usual" and trusting professional educators and parents in ways not even considered under many contemporary reform proposals and our pervasive, "usual" Model I ways of doing things. To try it seriously means accepting on a broad front the kinds of beliefs and attitudes we recommended for facilitators. To try it seriously means those in traditional power positions in schools, districts, state departments of education, governors' offices, and legislatures will need to trust those in the field to improve education and give them adequate time to develop, implement, assess, and revise action alternatives. To try it seriously means that academics in professional preparation programs need to relinquish control over the learning process by becoming less didactic and information oriented and more focused on the link between the classroom and the world of practice. Ironically, we cannot mandate reflection, no more than we can mandate collaborative decision making. What we can do is to provide the space, time, and support for those who already have the volition to try it. Certainly this nation could afford and profit from some genuine "experiments" in reflection as a means of change and improvement.

We seek colleagues who will join us in this "quiet" approach to change, who will move to the frontier that awaits us in almost every school and university in this nation, who are willing to risk so as to grow and improve our own professional practice while working with others to improve themselves. If we have learned anything in our personal journeys with reflective practice, it is that only through changing ourselves do we have any hope of changing others. That simple and overlooked truth is at the very center of becoming reflective practitioners. We seek colleagues who are prepared to risk changing.

References

Argyris, C. (1990). *Overcoming organizational defenses: Facilitating organizational learning*. Needham, MA: Allyn & Bacon.

Argyris, C., & Schon, D. A. (1974). *Theory in practice: Increasing professional effectiveness*. San Francisco: Jossey-Bass.

Babad, E., Bernieri, F., & Rosenthal, R. (1991). Students as judges of teachers' verbal and nonverbal behavior. *American Educational Research Journal, 28*(1), 211-234.

Barnett, B. G. (1990). Peer-assisted leadership: Expanding principals' knowledge through reflective practice. *Journal of Educational Administration, 28*(3), 67-76.

Barnett, B. G., & Brill, A. D. (1989, October). *Building reflection into administrative training programs*. Paper presented at the convention of the University Council for Educational Administration, Cincinnati.

Barth, R. (1990). *Improving schools from within*. San Francisco: Jossey-Bass.

Beebe, S. A., & Masterson, J. T. (1990). *Communicating in small groups: Principles and practices*. Glenview, IL: Scott, Foresman/Little, Brown Higher Education.

Belenky, M. F., Clinchy, B. M., Goldberger, N. R., & Tarule, J. M. (1986). *Women's ways of knowing: The development of self, voice, and mind*. New York: Basic Books.

Bennis, W. G., Benne, K. D., & Chin, R. (Eds.). (1961). *The planning of change*. New York: Holt, Rinehart & Winston.

Berkey, R., Campbell, D., Curtis, T., Kirschner, B. W., Minnick, F., & Zietlow, K. (1990). Collaborating for reflective practice: Voices of teachers, administrators, and researchers. *Education and Urban Society, 22*(2), 204-232.

Berlak, A., & Berlak, H. (1981). *Dilemmas of schooling*. New York: Methuen.

Bifano, S. L. (1989). Researching the professional practice of elementary principals: Combining quantitative methods and case study. *Journal of Educational Administration, 27*(1), 58-70.

Blase, J., & Kirby, P. C. (1992). *Bringing out the best in teachers*. Newbury Park, CA: Corwin.

Bolman, L. G., & Deal, T. E. (1991). *Reframing organizations: Artistry, choice, and leadership*. San Francisco: Jossey-Bass.

Bolton, R. (1979). *People skills: How to assert yourself, listen to others, and resolve conflicts*. New York: Simon & Schuster.

Bossert, S. T., Dwyer, D. C., Rowan, B., & Lee, V. G. (1982). The instructional management role of the principal. *Educational Administration Quarterly, 18*(3), 34-64.

Bridges, E. M. (1986). *The incompetent teacher*. Philadelphia: Falmer.

Bridges, E. M. (1992). *Problem-based learning for administrators*. Eugene, OR: ERIC Clearinghouse on Educational Management.

Brookfield, S. (1992). Uncovering assumptions: The key to reflective practice. *Adult Learning, 3*(4), 13-18.

Brown, J. S., Collins, A., & Duguid, P. (1989a). Debating the situation: A rejoinder to Palincsar and Wineburg. *Educational Researcher, 19*(4), 10-12.

Brown, J. S., Collins, A., & Duguid, P. (1989b). Situated cognition and the culture of learning. *Educational Researcher, 18*(1), 32-42.

Bruner, J. (1963). *The process of education*. New York: Vintage.

Budner, S. (1962). Intolerance of ambiguity as a personality variable. *Journal of Personality, 30*(1), 29-50.

Burns, T., & Stalker, G. M. (1961). *The management of innovation*. London: Tavistock.

Clandinin, D. J., & Connelly, F. M. (1991). Narrative and story in practice and research. In D. A. Schon (Ed.), *The reflective turn* (pp. 258-281). New York: Teachers College Press.

Clift, R. T., Houston, W. R., & Pugach, M. C. (1990). *Encouraging reflective practice in education*. New York: Teachers College Press.

Cohn, M. M., & Kottkamp, R. B. (1992). *Teachers: The missing voice in education.* Albany: State University of New York Press.

Cohn, M. M., & Lenz, O. V. (1990, April). *A systemic approach to school improvement: An inside/outside look at the Vertical Team Concept as a vehicle for change.* Paper presented at the annual meeting of the American Educational Research Association, Boston.

Connell, J. P., & Wellborn, J. G. (1989, April). *Competence, autonomy, and relatedness.* Paper presented at the annual meeting of the American Educational Research Association, San Francisco, CA.

Cuban, L. (1984). *How teachers taught: Constancy and change in American classrooms 1890-1980.* New York: Longman.

Cummins, J. (1986). Empowering minority students: A framework for intervention. *Harvard Educational Review, 56*(1), 18-36.

deCharms, R. (1968). *Personal causation: The internal affective determinants of behavior.* New York: Academic Press.

deCharms, R. (1976). *Enhancing motivation.* New York: Irvington.

deCharms, R. (1984). Motivation enhancement in educational settings. In R. Ames & C. Ames (Eds.), *Research on motivation in education* (pp. 275-308). New York: Academic Press.

Deci, E. L., & Ryan, R. M. (1985). *Intrinsic motivation and self determination in human behavior.* New York: Plenum.

Dewey, J. (1938a). *Experience and education.* New York: Macmillan.

Dewey, J. (1938b). *Logic: The theory of inquiry.* New York: Holt.

Doyle, M., & Straus, D. (1982). *How to make meetings work.* New York: Jove.

Emig, J. A. (1977). Writing as a mode of learning. *College Composition and Communication, 28*(2), 122-128.

Firestone, W. A., & Corbett, H. D. (1988). Planned organizational change. In N. J. Boyan (Ed.), *Handbook of research on educational administration* (pp. 321-340). New York: Longman.

Fulwiler, T. (Ed.). (1987). *The journal book.* Portsmouth, NH: Boynton/Cook.

Getzels, J. W. (1979). Problem-finding and research in educational administration. In G. L. Immegart & W. L. Boyd (Eds.), *Problem-finding in educational administration* (pp. 5-22). Lexington, MA: Lexington.

Gibb, J. (1961). Defensive communication. *Journal of Communication, 11*(3), 141-148.

Gitlin, A., & Bullough, R., Jr. (1989). Teacher evaluation and empowerment: Challenging the taken-for-granted view of teaching. In L. Weis, P. G. Altbach, G. T. Kelly, H. G. Petrie, & S. Slaughter (Eds.), *Crisis in teaching: Perspectives on current reform*. Albany: State University of New York Press.

Gitlin, A., & Smyth, J. (1989). *Teacher evaluation: Educative alternatives*. New York: Falmer.

Goodlad, J. (1984). *A place called school: Prospects for the future*. New York: McGraw-Hill.

Gordon, T. (1980). *Leader effectiveness training*. New York: Bantam.

Greenfield, T. B. (1986). The decline and fall of science in educational administration. *Interchange, 17*(2), 57-80.

Greenfield, T. (1991). Re-forming and re-valuing educational administration: When and when cometh the phoenix? *Educational Management and Administration, 19*(4), 200-217.

Griffiths, D. E. (1979). Another look at research on the behavior of administrators. In G. L. Immegart & W. L. Boyd (Eds.), *Problem-finding in educational administration* (pp. 41-62). Lexington, MA: D. C. Heath.

Grimmett, P. P., & Erickson, G. L. (Eds.). (1988). *Reflection in teacher education*. New York: Teachers College Press.

Holly, M. L. (1989). *Writing to grow: Keeping a personal-professional journal*. Portsmouth, NH: Heinemann.

Homans, G. C. (1950). *The human group*. New York: Harcourt, Brace, and World.

House, E. R. (1981). Three perspectives on educational innovation: Technological, political and cultural. In R. Lehming & M. Kane (Eds.), *Improving schools: Using what we know*. Beverly Hills, CA: Sage.

Jentz, B. (1982). *The hiring, start-up, and supervision of administrators*. New York: McGraw-Hill.

Jentz, B. C., & Wofford, J. W. (1979). *Leadership and learning*. New York: McGraw-Hill.

Johnson, D. W., & Johnson, F. P. (1991). *Joining together* (4th ed.). Englewood Cliffs, NJ: Prentice-Hall.

Johnson, D. W., & Johnson, R. (1989). *Cooperation and competition: Theory and research*. Edina, MN: Interaction Book Company.

Johnston, C. A. (1985). *The effects of training in transactional analysis upon the interpersonal communication transactions of graduate students in supervision.* Unpublished doctoral dissertation, Rutgers University.

Johnston, C. A. (1992). *Empowering the organization through professional talk.* Dubuque, IA: Kendall-Hunt.

Kelsey, J. G. T. (in press). Learning from teaching: Problems, problem-formulation and the enhancement of problem-solving capability. In P. Hallinger, K. A. Leithwood, & J. Murphy (Eds.), *A cognitive perspective on educational administration.* New York: Teachers College Press.

Kolb, D. A. (1984). *Experiential learning: Experience as the source of learning and development.* Englewood Cliffs, NJ: Prentice-Hall.

Kolb, D. A. (1985). *The learning style inventory: Technical manual.* Boston: McBer.

Kolbe, K. (1990). *The conative connection.* Reading, MA: Addison-Wesley.

Kottkamp, R. B. (1982). The administrative platform in administrative preparation. *Planning and Changing, 13*(2), 82-92.

Kottkamp, R. B. (1990a). Means for facilitating reflection. *Education and Urban Society, 22*(2), 182-203.

Kottkamp, R. B. (1990b, April). *The administrative platform as a means of reflection: A ten year assessment.* Paper presented at the annual meeting of the American Educational Research Association, Boston.

Leithwood, K., & Jantzi, D. (1990, April). *Transformational leadership: How principals can help reform school cultures.* Paper presented at the annual meeting of the American Educational Research Association, Boston.

Likert, R. (1961). *New patterns of management.* New York: McGraw-Hill.

Malen, B., Ogawa, R. T., & Kranz, J. (1990). What do we know about school-based management? A case study of the literature: A call for research. In W. H. Clune & J. Witte (Eds.), *Choice and control in American education* (pp. 289-342). London: Falmer.

Mattingly, C. (1991). Narrative reflections on practical actions: Two learning experiments in reflective storytelling. In D. A. Schon (Ed.), *The reflective turn* (pp. 235-257). New York: Teachers College Press.

McGregor, D. (1960). *The human side of enterprise.* New York: McGraw-Hill.

McLaughlin, M. W., & Pfeiffer, R. S. (1988). *Teacher evaluation: Improvement, accountability, and effective learning.* New York: Teachers College Press.

Miller, J. L. (1988). The resistance of women academics: An autobiographical account. In W. F. Pinar (Ed.), *Contemporary curriculum discourses* (pp. 486-494). Scottsdale, AZ: Gorsuch Scaribrick.

Miller, J. L. (1990a). *Creating spaces and finding voices: Teachers collaborating for empowerment.* Albany: State University of New York Press.

Miller, J. L. (1990b). Teachers as curriculum creators. In J. Sears & J. D. Marshall (Eds.), *Teaching and thinking about curriculum: Critical inquiries* (pp. 85-96). New York: Teachers College Press.

Myers, I. B., & McCaulley, M. H. (1985). *Manual: A guide to the development and use of the Myers-Briggs Type Indicator.* Palo Alto, CA: Consulting Psychologists Press.

National Public Radio. (1991, January 24). *All things considered.* Washington, DC: Author.

Natriello, G., & Dornbusch, S. M. (1984). *Teacher evaluative standards and student effort.* New York: Longman.

Osterman, K. F. (1990). Reflective practice: A new agenda for education. *Education and Urban Society, 22*(2), 133-152.

Osterman, K. F. (1991). Case records: A means to enhance the knowledge base in educational administration. In F. C. Wendel (Ed.), *Enhancing the knowledge base in educational administration* (pp. 35-47). University Park, PA: University Council for Educational Administration.

Osterman, K. F., & Sullivan, S. M. (1992, April). *Individualization, collaboration, and reflection: A different route to principal renewal.* Paper presented at the annual convention of the American Association for School Administrators, San Diego, CA.

Parkay, F. W., & Hall, G. E. (1992). *Becoming a principal: The challenges of beginning leadership.* Needham Heights, MA: Allyn & Bacon.

Past and future of the nation's report card. (1991, Fall/Winter). *OERI Bulletin,* pp. 1-2.

Peters, T. J., & Waterman, R. H. (1982). *In search of excellence.* New York: Harper & Row.

Prestine, N. A., & LeGrand, B. F. (1991). Cognitive learning theory and the preparation of educational administrators: Implications for practice and policy. *Educational Administration Quarterly, 27*(1), 61-89.

Progoff, I. (1975). *At a journal workshop*. New York: Dialogue House.

Roderich, J. A. (1986). Dialogue writing: Context for reflecting on self as teacher and researcher. *Journal of Curriculum and Supervision, 1,* 305-335.

Sagor, R. D. (1991, October). *Operationalizing transformational leadership: The behavior of principals in fostering teacher centered school development*. Paper presented at the Annual Conference of the University Council for Educational Administration, Baltimore, MD.

Sarason, S. B. (1971). *The culture of the school and the problem of change*. Boston: Allyn & Bacon.

Sarason, S. B. (1990). *The predictable failure of educational reform: Can we change course before it's too late?* San Francisco: Jossey-Bass.

Schmuck, P., & Schmuck, R. (1990). Democratic participation in small-town schools. *Educational Researcher, 19*(8), 14-19.

Schmuck, R. A., & Runkel, P. J. (1972). *Handbook of organizational development in schools*. Palo Alto, CA: Mayfield.

Schon, D. A. (1983). *The reflective practitioner: How professionals think in action*. New York: Basic Books.

Schon, D. A. (1987). *Educating the reflective practitioner*. San Francisco: Jossey-Bass.

Senge, P. M. (1990). The leader's new work: Building learning organizations. *Sloan Management Review, 32*(1), 7-23.

Sergiovanni, T. J. (1991). Contructing and changing theories of practice: The key to preparing school administrators. *Urban Review, 23*(1), 39-49.

Sergiovanni, T. J., & Starratt, R. J. (1983). *Supervision: Human perspectives* (3rd ed.). New York: McGraw-Hill.

Silver, P. F. (1986). Case records: A reflective practice approach to administrator development. *Theory into Practice, 25*(3), 161-167.

Weber, M. (1947). *The theory of social and economic organization*. New York: Free Press.

Wise, A. E. (1979). *Legislated learning: The bureaucratization of the American classroom*. Berkeley: University of California Press.

Wise, A. E. (1988). Two conflicting trends in school reform: Legislated learning revisited. *Phi Delta Kappan, 69*(5), 328-333.

Index

Printed in the United States
4825